W. Burstow 10-1-97

How To Say It

▲ENGLISH ▲TIGRINYA ▲ITALIAN

The royalties from this book will be used to support Bana's projects in Eritrea, and will be matched by the publisher.

BANA
(Light Beam)

Under this name resounds the voice of a thousand Eritrean Women, Ex-combatants, who fought heroically in the 30 year struggle for independence, but then found themselves unskilled and unemployed in peacetime society.

Most of the women are single supporting mothers. Although they received severance pay from the government following demobilization, this could not meet their subsistence needs. Faced with the new challenge, the women decided to combine their resources and founded the 'BANA SHARE COMPANY', in 1995.

One of the main objectives of the company is the creation of secure employment for all its members. Bana has launched a variety of projects, ranging from fish-market and bakery cooperatives, to support for women's employment in the construction sector. Over two hundred women have already been trained in driving, carpentry, catering, fish-processing, computing and in the construction trade.

Now Bana is planning to establish an Editorial and Publishing Unit, also run by its members. The aim is not only to offer new skilled work opportunities, but to give voice to women's issues in Eritrea. Bana hopes to promote, through this important communications project, the increasing participation of women in the economic and political development of the country.

Bana gratefully acknowledges all the local and international assistance received in the making of this book, the proceeds from which will go towards funding Bana's activities.

Further contributions - whether moral support, donations or expertise - would be greatly appreciated. The contact address is:

BANA
SHARE COMPANY
(Eritrean Demobilized Female Fighters Association)

Ruth Simon
Chairwoman
Bana Share Company
P O Box 4923
Asmara, Eritrea
Tel. & Fax : 291 1 12 24 62

How To Say It

▲ENGLISH ▲TIGRINYA ▲ITALIAN

ENGLISH

ትግርኛ

ITALIANO

LEONARDO ORIOLO
AMANUEL SAHLE
SENAIT IYOB

The Red Sea Press, Inc.
Publishers & Distributors of Third World Books
RSP
11-D Princess Road
Lawrenceville, NJ 08648
P. O. Box 48
Asmara, ERITREA

The Red Sea Press, Inc.
Publishers & Distributors of Third World Books

11-D Princess Road
Lawrenceville, NJ 08648

P. O. Box 48
Asmara, ERITREA

First Printing 1997

Copyright © 1997 Leonardo Oriolo

All rights reserved. No part of this publication may be reproduced, stored in a retrieval system or transmitted in any form or by any means electronic, mechanical, photocopying, recording or otherwise without the prior written permission of the publisher.

Book design: Leonardo Oriolo
Cover design: Linda Nickens

Library of Congress Cataloging-in-Publication Data
Oriolo, Leonardo.
How to say it in English, Tigrinya, Italian / [Leonardo Oriolo, Amanuel Sahle, Senait Iyob].
p. cm.
English, Italian, and Tigrinya.
ISBN 1-56902-054-X (paper : alk.paper). -- ISBN 1-56902-055-8 (cassette). -- ISBN 1-56902-056-6 (package)
1. Tigrinya language--Conversation and phrase books--English.
2. Tigrinya language--Conversation and phrase books--Italian.
3. English language--Conversation and phrase books--Tigrinya.
4. English language--Conversation and phrase books--Italian.
5. Italian language--Conversation and phrase books--Tigrinya.
6. Italian language--Conversation and phrase books--English.
I. Amanuel Sahle. II. Senait Iyob. III. Title.
PJ9111.075 1997
418--dc21 97-2021
CIP

ACKNOWLEDGEMENTS

The author would like to thank the following:
Amanuel Sahle and Senait Iyob who translated the 'English-Italian manuscript' into Tigrinya and made many helpful suggestions; Maurizio Semolic for assisting in the layout and artwork; Claudia Costa, Selomé Iyob, Miriam Haile and Sami Sallinen for their invaluable help during the writing of the book; Ruth Simon, Miriam Mareso and Celina Fernandes for their meticulous proof-reading; Nicocia Onofrio for permission to reproduce the illustration on p. x.
I would also like to thank the following for taking part in the recording: Anna Martini, Antonella Ferrando, Angelo Modici, Guido Traverso, Ross Hughes, Sandrine Tiller, Solomon Abera, Stephen Nelson, Tiziana Belluco e Weini Gherezghiher.
Finally I should like to join Bana S.C. in expressing our gratitude for the considerable support offered by the publisher Kassahun Checole.

The clipart images incorporated into the publication are from Corel GALLERY 2. Corel® is a registered trademark of Corel Corporation.

The author apologises if any acknowledgements have been omitted and will be pleased to include them in subsequent editions.

L.O.

CONTENTS

INTRODUCTORY NOTE

The main purpose of *How to say it ...* is to provide essential practice material in an accessible form for developing the learner's ability to communicate effectively in English, Tigrinya or Italian.
Constant practice and exposure are indispensable factors in learning a language, as are motivation and enjoyment. To develop and strengthen the communication resources of the learner, this book presents, and repeats cyclically, the most relevant language functions and notions. This 'spiral system' of presenting material is the distinguishing feature of the book.

The book provides:
• Lists of language tasks presented according to the topics and settings in which they may occur.
• Phraseology - referring to the lists of language tasks - covering most of the vocabulary, structures, notions and functions to be used productively and receptively.
The phraseology generally follows the pattern of a conversation, presenting questions on the left-hand side and answers on the right-hand side.
• Main linguistic functions.
• Substitution tables.
• Vocabulary lists by topic.
The main topics are: Personal Identification, Family, House and Home, Geographical Surroundings and Weather, Travel and Transport, Holidays, Accommodation, Food and Drink, Shopping, Services, Health, Free Time, Education.

A WORD ON TIGRINYA

Tigrinya is a Semitic language spoken in the Eritrean Highlands, most of Tigray and parts of Wollo and Gonder (Northern Ethiopia). It is the fourth widely spoken Semitic language in the world after Arabic, Hebrew and Amharic.
Tigrinya as a spoken language has been in existence since the 13th century, but it developed, in its written form, only after the beginning of the 19th century.
The Tigrinya variation adopted in this book is the one spoken in Asmara - the capital of Eritrea - and used by the Eritrean mass media.

TO THE TEACHER

The following points suggest ways of exploiting the material in class to ensure that the target language becomes the normal means of communication during the lessons (some stages can be omitted if circumstances allow).

1. The teacher presents the list of language tasks.
2. Students look at pictures relating to the subject being discussed and try to answer simple questions (Who? What? Where? ...).
3. Students listen to the text, without looking at it. The teacher can either use the cassette or read a short dialogue based on the phraseology - questions and answers- or on the substitution tables.
4. Explanation (using, where possible, pictures and/or mime).
5. Spoken comprehension questions (listening again to short phrases).

6. Chorus work (for pronunciation and intonation practice).
7. Teacher asks students questions (using (A) column).
8. Students try to answer in chorus (book closed but with stimulus from pictures or from teacher's gestures).
9. Teacher repeats the answers.

10. Teacher gives answers (this time using (B) column).
11. Students ask questions (book closed).
12. Teacher repeats questions.

13. Students listen again to short opening dialogue, this time reading the text.
14. Students work in pairs as in 7, 8, 9, 10 with the help of the text and, taking turns to cover 'A' and 'B' columns.
15. Students work in pairs and act out the dialogue (with visual aids).
16. Students in pairs make up their own dialogue, with the help of the substitution tables and of the vocabulary list by topics.
17. Students and teacher discuss the dialogue, adding extra phrases where suitable and, at an early stage, correcting only mistakes which interfere with communication.
18. Students work in pairs practising the dialogue and then acting it out in front of the class (it's useful to record these dialogues and to listen to them afterwards).

19. Students exchange their proposed dialogues and do as in 18 above.
20. Students think about and revise the different structures learnt.

Useful words in the classroom

Listen/Look	*ascoltate/osservate*	Listen and Write	*ascoltate e scrivete*
Ask	*domandate*	Listen and Read	*ascoltate e leggete*
Write/Read	*scrivete/leggete*	Listen and Repeat	*ascoltate e ripetete*
True or False	*vero o falso*	Listen to the tape	*ascoltate la cassetta*
Yes or No	*sì o no*	Ask questions	*fate le domande*
Invent/Guess	*inventate/indovinate*	Answer the questions	*rispondete alle domande*

Illustration (page 1): "ERITREA" by Onofrio Nicocia

ERITREA
ኤርትራ
ارتريا
أونوفريو

1 PERSONAL IDENTIFICATION

How to give and ask information about ...
1. Name
2. Home address
3. Telephone number
4. Age
5. Nationality
6. Likes and dislikes

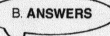

A. **QUESTIONS**	B. **ANSWERS**
1.1 What's [What is] your name?	1.2 (My name is) Mary. 1.3 (My name is) Charles.
2.1 What's your address?	2.2 (My address is) 5, Market Street.
3.1 What's your telephone number?	3.2 (My telephone number is) 340 1256.

What's your name?
My name is Mary.

ውልቃዊ ሓበሬታ

ከመይ ጌርካ ሓበሬታ ትህብን ትሓትትን
1. ስም
2. ኣድራሻ
3. ቍጽሪ ቴሌፎን
4. ዕድመ
5. ዜግነት
6. እትፈትዎን እትጸልኦን

1.1 መን ኢዩ ስምኪ፧ (f)
መን ኢዩ ስምካ፧ (m)

1.2 ስመይ ምርያም ኢዩ
1.3 ስመይ ካርሎ ኢዩ

2.1 ኣድራሻኻ ኣበይ'ዩ፧ (m)
ኣድራሻኺ ኣበይ'ዩ፧ (f)

2.2 ጎደና ዕዳጋ ቁ. 5 ኢዩ

3.1 ቍጽሪ ስልክኻ ክንደይ'ዩ፧ (m)
ቍጽሪ ስልክኺ ክንደይ'ዩ፧ (f)

3.2 ቍጽሪ ስልከይ 340 1256 ኢዩ

IDENTIFICAZIONE PERSONALE

Come dare e chiedere informazioni su ...
1. il nome
2. l'indirizzo
3. il numero di telefono
4. l'età
5. la nazionalità
6. le preferenze

1.1 Come ti chiami?

1.2 (Mi chiamo) Maria.
1.3 (Mi chiamo) Carlo.

2.1 Qual è il tuo indirizzo?

2.2 (Il mio indirizzo è) Via del Mercato, n. 5.

3.1 Qual è il tuo numero di telefono?

3.2 (Il mio numero di telefono è) 340 12 56.

4.1 How old are you?	4.4 I'm fourteen. 4.5 I'm fifteen. 4.6 I'm sixteen.
4.2 When were you born ?	4.7 (I was born) on the 2nd of January 1974.
4.3 When is your birthday?	4.8 The 3rd of February. 4.9 The 4th of March.
5.1 What nationality are you?	5.8 I'm English. 5.9 I'm Italian. 5.10 I'm American. 5.11 I'm Eritrean.
5.2 Are you Italian? 5.3 Is he/she English? 5.4 Are you Italian? 5.5 Are they English?	5.12 No, I'm Spanish. 5.13 No, he/she is American. 5.14 No, we are Spanish. 5.15 No, they are American.

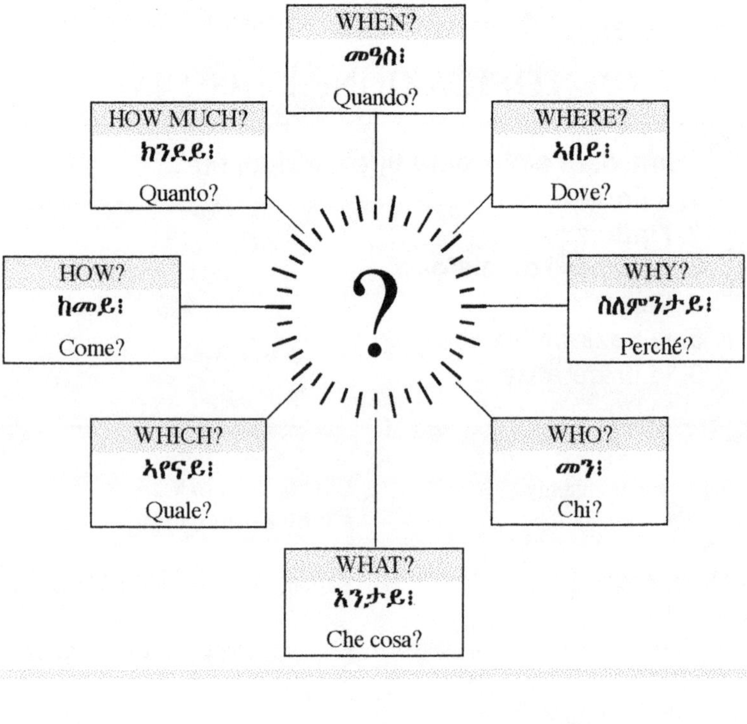

4.1 ክንደይ ኢዩ ዕድመኻ፧ (m)
ክንደይ ኢዩ ዕድመኺ፧ (f)

4.4 ወዲ/ጓል 14 ዓመት እየ
4.5 ወዲ/ጓል 15 ዓመት እየ
4.6 ወዲ/ጓል 16 ዓመት እየ

4.2 መዓስ ተወሊድካ፧ (m)
መዓስ ተወሊድኪ፧ (f)

4.7 ጥሪ፡ 2፡ 1974

4.3 ዕለተ ልደትካ መዓስ ኢዩ፧ (m)
ዕለተ ልደትኪ መዓስ ኢዩ፧ (f)

4.8 3 የካቲት
4.9 4 መጋቢት

5.1 ዜግነትካ እንታይ ኢዩ፧
ዜግነትኪ እንታይ ኢዩ፧

5.8 እንግሊዛዊ/ት እየ
5.9 ኢጣልያዊ/ት እየ
5.10 ኣመሪካዊ/ት እየ
5.11 ኤርትራዊ/ት እየ

5.2 ኢጣልያዊ ዲኻ/ ኢጣልያዊት ዲኺ፧
5.3 እንግሊዛዊ ዲዩ/ እንግሊዛዊት ዲያ፧
5.4 ኢጣልያውያን ዲኹም/ ዲኽን፧
5.5 እንግሊዛውያን ዲዮም/ ዲየን፧

5.12 ኣይፋልን፡ እስጳኛዊ/ት እየ
5.13 ኣይፋልን፡ ኣመሪካዊ/ት ኢዩ/ኢያ
5.14 ኣይፋልን፡ እስጳኛውያን ኢና
5.15 ኣይፋልን፡ ኣመሪካውያን ኢዮም/ ኢየን

4.1 Quanti anni hai?

4.4 Ho quattordici anni.
4.5 Ho quindici anni.
4.6 Ho sedici anni.

4.2 Quando sei nato? (m)
Quando sei nata? (f)

4.7 (Sono nato) il 2 gennaio 1974.
(Sono nata) il 2 gennaio 1974.

4.3 Quando è il tuo compleanno?

4.8 Il 3 febbraio.
4.9 Il 4 marzo.

5.1 Di che nazionalità sei?

5.8 Sono inglese.
5.9 Sono italiano/a.
5.10 Sono americano/a.
5.11 Sono eritreo/a.

5.2 Sei italiano/a?
5.3 È inglese?
5.4 Siete italiani/e?
5.5 Sono inglesi?

5.12 No, sono spagnolo/a.
5.13 No, è americano/a.
5.14 No, siamo spagnoli/e.
5.15 No, sono americani/e.

5.6 Where were you born?	5.16 (I was born) in Mendefera. 5.17 (I was born) in Dekemhare. 5.18 (I was born) in Italy. 5.19 (I was born) in England.
5.7 Where are you from?	5.20 I'm from England. 5.21 I'm from Italy. 5.22 I'm from the United States. 5.23 I'm from Eritrea.
6.1 Do you like Italian? 6.2 Do you like this book? 6.3 Do you like this pen?	6.6 Yes, I do [I like it].
6.4 Do you like these books? 6.5 Do you like these pens?	6.7 Yes, I do [I like them]. 6.8 No, I prefer these (pens).

5.6 ኣበይ ተወሊድካ/ኪ፧	5.16 ኣብ መንደፈራ ተወሊደ 5.17 ኣብ ደቀምሓረ ተወሊደ 5.18 ኣብ ዓዲ ጥልያን ተወሊደ 5.19 ኣብ ዓዲ እንግሊዝ ተወሊደ
5.7 ካበይ መጺእካ/ኪ፧	5.20 ካብ ዓዲ እንግሊዝ እየ 5.21 ካብ ዓዲ ጥልያን እየ 5.22 ካብ ሕቡራት መንግስታት ኣመሪካ እየ 5.23 ካብ ኤርትራ እየ
6.1 ጥልያን ይፍተወካዶ/ ጥልያን ይፍተወኪዶ፧ 6.2 እዚኣ መጽሓፍ ትፍተወካዶ/ እዚኣ መጽሓፍ ትፍተወኪዶ፧ 6.3 እዚኣ ቢሮ ትፍተወካዶ/ እዚኣ ቢሮ ትፍተወኪዶ፧	6.6 እወ፡ እፈትዋ እየ
6.4 እዘን መጽሓፍቲ ይፍተዋኻዶ/ እዘን መጽሓፍቲ ይፍተዋኺዶ፧ 6.5 እዘን ቢሮታት ይፍተዋኻዶ/ ይፍተዋኺዶ፧	6.7 እወ፡ እፈትወን እየ 6.8 ኣይፋልን፡ ነዘን ቢሮታት እመርጽ

INFORMALE (tu)	FORMALE (Lei)
Ciao!	Buongiorno!
Come ti chiami?	Come si chiama?
Ti presento Franco.	Le presento il signor Marconi.
Di che nazionalità sei?	Di che nazionalità è?
Di dove sei?	Di dove è?
Parli italiano?	Parla italiano?
Come stai?	Come sta?
Non c'è male. E tu?	Non c'è male. E lei?
Qual è il tuo indirizzo?	Qual è il suo indirizzo?
Quando è il tuo compleanno?	Quando è il suo compleanno?
Quanti anni hai?	Quanti anni ha?
Sei sposato?	E' sposato?
Ti piace l'italiano?	Le piace l'italiano?

5.6 Dove sei nato?
Dove sei nata?

5.16 Sono nato/a a Mendefera.
5.17 Sono nato/a a Dekemhare.
5.18 Sono nato/a in Italia.
5.19 Sono nato/a in Inghilterra.

5.7 Da dove vieni?

5.20 (Vengo) dall'Inghilterra.
5.21 (Vengo) dall'Italia.
5.22 (Vengo) dagli Stati Uniti.
5.23 (Vengo) dall'Eritrea.

6.1 Ti piace l'italiano?
6.2 Ti piace questo libro?
6.3 Ti piace questa penna?

6.6 Sì, mi piace.

6.4 Ti piacciono questi libri?
6.5 Ti piacciono queste penne?

6.7 Sì, mi piacciono.
6.8 No, preferisco queste (penne).

Numbers

ኣሃዛት

Numeri

1 one	11 eleven	21 twenty-one	40 forty
2 two	12 twelve	22 twenty-two	50 fifty
3 three	13 thirteen	23 twenty-three	60 sixty
4 four	14 fourteen	24 twenty-four	70 seventy
5 five	15 fifteen	25 twenty-five	80 eighty
6 six	16 sixteen	26 twenty-six	90 ninety
7 seven	17 seventeen	27 twenty-seven	100 a/one hundred
8 eight	18 eighteen	28 twenty-eight	200 two hundred
9 nine	19 nineteen	29 twenty-nine	1,000 a/one thousand
10 ten	20 twenty	30 thirty	1,000,000 a/one million

1 ሓደ	11 ዓሰርተው ሓደ	21 ዕስራን ሓደን	40 ኣርባዓ
2 ክልተ	12 ዓሰርተው ክልተ	22 ዕስራን ክልተን	50 ሓምሳ
3 ሰለስተ	13 ዓሰርተው ሰለስተ	23 ዕስራን ሰለስተን	60 ስሳ
4 ኣርባዕተ	14 ዓሰርተው ኣርባዕተ	24 ዕስራን ኣርባዕተን	70 ሰብዓ
5 ሓሙሽተ	15 ዓሰርተው ሓሙሽተ	25 ዕስራን ሓሙሽተን	80 ሰማንያ
6 ሽድሽተ	16 ዓሰርተው ሽድሽተ	26 ዕስራን ሽድሽተን	90 ተስዓ
7 ሸውዓተ/ሸብዓተ	17 ዓሰርተው ሸብዓተ	27 ዕስራን ሸብዓተን	100 ሚእቲ
8 ሸሞንተ	18 ዓሰርተው ሸሞንተ	28 ዕስራን ሸሞንተን	200 ክልተ ሚእቲ
9 ትሽዓተ	19 ዓሰርተው ትሽዓተ	29 ዕስራን ትሽዓተን	1.000 ሽሕ
10 ዓሰርተ	20 ዕስራ	30 ሰላሳ	1.000.000 ሚልዮን

1 uno	11 undici	21 ventuno	40 quaranta
2 due	12 dodici	22 ventidue	50 cinquanta
3 tre	13 tredici	23 ventitré	60 sessanta
4 quattro	14 quattordici	24 ventiquattro	70 settanta
5 cinque	15 quindici	25 venticinque	80 ottanta
6 sei	16 sedici	26 ventisei	90 novanta
7 sette	17 diciassette	27 ventisette	100 cento
8 otto	18 diciotto	28 ventotto	200 duecento
9 nove	19 diciannove	29 ventinove	1.000 mille
10 dieci	20 venti	30 trenta	1.000.000 un milione

How to describe a person
ንሰብ ከመይ ትገልጾ
Come descrivere una persona

1. Who?	Charles, Mary, David, ...
2. Age	He/She is ... (years old).
3. Height	Tall, short, medium height, ...
4. Build	Thin, fat, robust/strong, slim, ...
5. Hair	• Long, short, ... • Brown, black/dark, blonde/fair, ... • Straight hair, curly hair, ...
6. Eyes	Hazel, light blue, green, ...
7. Dress	Sporty/casual (wear), elegant/smart, ...
8. Character	Cheerful, good, calm, amusing, happy, kind, intelligent, nervous, honest, lazy, strict, lively, unpleasant, nice, ...
9. Occupation	Driver, waiter, housewife, shop-assistant, dentist, manager, unemployed, male nurse, butcher, teacher (primary), mechanic, doctor, policeman, teacher, secretary, student, ...

1. መን፧	ካርሎ፡ ምርያም፡ ዳዊት፡ ...
2. ዕድመ	... ዓመት ኣለዎ / ... ዓመት ኣለዋ
3. ቍመት	ነዊሕ፡ ሓጺር፡ ማእከላይ፡ ...
4. ቍመና	ቀጢን፡ ስቡሕ፡ ድልዱል፡ ምልምል፡ ...
5. ጸጕሪ ርእሲ	ነዊሕ፡ ሓጺር፡ ቡናዊ፡ ጸሊም፡ በሓይ፡ ለማሽ፡ ርሽርሽ፡ ...
6. ኣዒንቲ	ቡናዊ፡ ሰማያዊ፡ ቀጠልያ፡ ...
7. ኣከዳድና	ስፖርታዊ፡ ኤለጋንተ፡ ...
8. ጠባይ	ሕጉስ፡ ንፉዕ፡ ህዱእ፡ ተዋዛያይ፡ ሕጉስ፡ ምቕሉል፡ በሊሕ፡ ሓራቕ፡ ቅኑዕ፡ ሃካይ፡ ተሪር፡ ውዑይ፡ ዘይፍተው፡ ፍቱው፡ ...
9. ስራሕ	መራሕ መኪና፡ ኣሰላፊ፡ በዓልቲ ሓዳር፡ ሰራሕተኛ ድኳን፡ ሓኪምስኒ፡ ዳይረክተር፡ ስራሕ ኣልቦ፡ ነርስ፡ ሽያጥስጋ፡ መምህር፡ ዓራይመኪና፡ ሓኪም፡ ፖሊስ፡ መምህር፡ ጸሓፊት፡ ተመሃራይ፡ ...

1. Chi?	Carlo, Maria, David, ...
2. Età	Ha ... anni.
3. Altezza	Alto, basso, di statura media, ...
4. Corporatura	Magro, grasso, robusto, snello, ...
5. Capelli	• Lunghi, corti, ... • Castani, neri, biondi, ... • Lisci, ricci, ...
6. Occhi	Castani, azzurri, verdi, ...
7. Abbigliamento	Sportivo, elegante, ...
8. Carattere	Allegro, bravo, calmo, divertente, felice, gentile, intelligente, nervoso, onesto, pigro, severo, vivace, antipatico, simpatico, ...
9. Mestieri e professioni	Autista, cameriere, casalinga, commesso, dentista, direttore, disoccupato, infermiere, macellaio, maestro, meccanico, medico, poliziotto, professore, segretario, studente, ...

TIGRINYA ALPHABET

1° Gheez	2° Caib	3° Salis	4° Rabi	5° Hamis	6° Sadis	7° Sabi
ሀ	ሁ	ሂ	ሃ	ሄ	ህ	ሆ
ለ	ሉ	ሊ	ላ	ሌ	ል	ሎ
ሐ	ሑ	ሒ	ሓ	ሔ	ሕ	ሖ
መ	ሙ	ሚ	ማ	ሜ	ም	ሞ
ረ	ሩ	ሪ	ራ	ሬ	ር	ሮ
ሰ	ሱ	ሲ	ሳ	ሴ	ስ	ሶ
ሸ	ሹ	ሺ	ሻ	ሼ	ሽ	ሾ
ቀ	ቁ	ቂ	ቃ	ቄ	ቅ	ቆ
በ	ቡ	ቢ	ባ	ቤ	ብ	ቦ
ተ	ቱ	ቲ	ታ	ቴ	ት	ቶ
ቸ	ቹ	ቺ	ቻ	ቼ	ች	ቾ
ነ	ኑ	ኒ	ና	ኔ	ን	ኖ
ኘ	ኙ	ኚ	ኛ	ኜ	ኝ	ኞ
አ	ኡ	ኢ	ኣ	ኤ	እ	ኦ
ከ	ኩ	ኪ	ካ	ኬ	ክ	ኮ
ወ	ዉ	ዊ	ዋ	ዌ	ው	ዎ
ዐ	ዑ	ዒ	ዓ	ዔ	ዕ	ዖ
ዘ	ዙ	ዚ	ዛ	ዜ	ዝ	ዞ
ዠ	ዡ	ዢ	ዣ	ዤ	ዥ	ዦ
የ	ዩ	ዪ	ያ	ዬ	ይ	ዮ
ደ	ዱ	ዲ	ዳ	ዴ	ድ	ዶ
ጀ	ጁ	ጂ	ጃ	ጄ	ጅ	ጆ
ገ	ጉ	ጊ	ጋ	ጌ	ግ	ጎ
ጠ	ጡ	ጢ	ጣ	ጤ	ጥ	ጦ
ጨ	ጩ	ጪ	ጫ	ጬ	ጭ	ጮ
ጸ	ጹ	ጺ	ጻ	ጼ	ጽ	ጾ
ፀ	ፁ	ፂ	ፃ	ፄ	ፅ	ፆ
ፈ	ፉ	ፊ	ፋ	ፌ	ፍ	ፎ
ፐ	ፑ	ፒ	ፓ	ፔ	ፕ	ፖ
ኸ	ኹ	ኺ	ኻ	ኼ	ኽ	ኾ
ቐ	ቑ	ቒ	ቓ	ቔ	ቕ	ቖ
ቨ	ቩ	ቪ	ቫ	ቬ	ቭ	ቮ
ኰ		ኲ	ኳ	ኴ	ኵ	
ዀ		ዂ	ዃ	ዄ	ዅ	
ቈ		ቊ	ቋ	ቌ	ቍ	
ቘ		ቚ	ቛ	ቜ	ቝ	
ጐ		ጒ	ጓ	ጔ	ጕ	

ENGLISH ALPHABET

A B C D E F G H I J K L M N O P Q R S T U V W X Y Z

ALFABETO ITALIANO

A B C D E F G H I L M N O P Q R S T U V Z (J K W X Y)

Key phrases	ኣገደስቲ ቃላት	Fraseologia essenziale
1. Do you speak English?	1. እንግሊዝ ትዛረብዶ፧	1. Parli inglese? Parla inglese? *
2. Not very well.	2. ብዙሕ ኣይኮነን	2. Non molto bene.
3. Can you repeat?	3. ክትደግሞ ትኽእልዶ፧	3. Potrebbe ripetere?
4. I don't understand.	4. ኣይተረደኣንን	4. Non capisco.
5. How do you say ...?	5. ... እንታይ ይብሃል፧	5. Come si dice ...?
6. How do you write ...?	6. ... ከመይ ይጽሓፍ፧	6. Come si scrive ...?
7. What does ... mean?	7. ... እንታይ ማለት ኢዩ፧	7. Che cosa vuol dire ...?
8. Excuse me!	8. ይቕረታ	8. Scusi?
9. I'm sorry.	9. ኣይትሓዘለይ	9. Mi dispiace.
10. Please.	10. በጃኻ	10. Per piacere.
11. Thank you.	11. የቐንየለይ	11. Grazie!
12. You're welcome.	12. ገንዘብካ	12. Prego!
13. How are you?	13. ከመይ ኣሎኻ/ ከመይ ትኸውን፧	13. Come stai? Come sta? *
14. Not bad.	14. ደሓን	14. Non c'è male.
15. Very well, thank you. And you?	15. ሰናይ፣ ንስኹም/ኽን ከ፧	15. Bene grazie e tu/Lei?
16. Not too good ...	16. ብዙሕ ጽቡቕ የለኹን	16. Non molto bene ...
17. Good morning.	17. ደሓንዶ ሓዲርኩም፧	17. Buongiorno.
18. Good evening.	18. ልዋም ምሸት	18. Buonasera.
19. Good night.	19. ልዋም ለይቲ	19. Buonanotte.
20. Good-bye.	20. ደሓን ኩኑ	20. Arrivederci.
21. Hello/Bye/See you!	21. ሰላም/ ደሓን ኩኑ/ ብደሓን የራኽበና	21. Ciao!
22. See you tomorrow.	22. ጽባሕ የራኽበና	22. A domani.
23. This is Mary.	23. እዚኣ ሜሪ ኢያ	23. Questa è Maria.
24. May I introduce Mr. Keith Willis?	24. ምስ ኣቶ ከይዝ ዊልስዶ ከፋልጠካ፧	24. Le presento il signor Marconi.
25. How do you do?	25. ከመይ ትኸውን፧	25. Piacere.
26. Pleased to meet you.	26. ጽቡቕ ሌላ ይግበረልና	26. Molto lieto (m) Molto lieta (f)

* Formale

2 FAMILY

HOW TO ...
Ask information about members of the family

1.1 How many are you in your family?
1.2 Are there many of you in your family?

1.25 There are four of us.

1.3 What's your father's name?
1.4 What is your grandfather's name?
1.5 What is your brother's name?
1.6 What is your uncle's name?
1.7 What is your cousin's name?
1.8 What is your son's name?
1.9 What is your husband's name?
1.10 What is your brother-in-law's name?
1.11 What is your nephew's name?
1.12 What is your father-in-law called?

1.26 (His name is) Charles.
He's [He is] called Charles.

ስድራቤት

ክመይ ጌርካ ...
ብዛዕባ ኣባላት ስድራቤት ሓበሬታ ክም እትሓትት

1.1 ኣባላት ስድራቤትኩም ክንደይ ኢዮም፧
1.2 ስድራቤትኩም ክንደይ ኢኹም፧

1.3 ኣቦኻ/ኺ መን ይብሃል፧
1.4 ኣቦሓጎኻ/ኺ መን ይብሃል፧
1.5 ሓውኻ/ኺ መን ይብሃል፧
1.6 ኣኮኻ/ኺ / ሓወቦኻ/ኺ መን ይብሃል፧
1.7 ወዲ ሓወቦኻ/ኺ፣ ወዲ ኣኮኻ/ኺ፣ ወዲ ኣሞኻ/ኺ፣ ወዲ ሓትንኻ/ኺ መን ይብሃል፧
1.8 ወድኻ/ኺ መን ይብሃል፧
1.9 በዓል ቤትኪ መን ይብሃል፧
1.10 ሰብኣይ ሓውትኻ/ኺ መን ይብሃል፧
1.11 ወዲ ሓውትኻ/ኺ፣ ሓውኻ/ኺ፣ መን ይብሃል፧
1.12 ሓሙኻ/ኺ መን ይብሃል፧

1.25 ኣርባዕተ ኢና

1.26 ካርሎ ይብሃል

FAMIGLIA

Come ...
chiedere informazioni sui componenti della famiglia

1.1 Quanti siete in famiglia?
1.2 Siete tanti in famiglia?

1.3 Come si chiama tuo padre ?
1.4 Come si chiama tuo nonno?
1.5 Come si chiama tuo fratello?
1.6 Come si chiama tuo zio?
1.7 Come si chiama tuo cugino?
1.8 Come si chiama tuo figlio?
1.9 Come si chiama tuo marito?
1.10 Come si chiama tuo cognato?
1.11 Come si chiama tuo nipote?
1.12 Come si chiama tuo suocero?

1.25 Siamo in quattro.

1.26 (Si chiama) Carlo.

1.12 What's your mother's name?
1.13 What is your grandmother's name?
1.14 What is your sister's name?
1.15 What is your aunt's name?
1.16 What is your cousin's name?
1.17 What is your daughter's name?
1.18 What is your wife's name?
1.19 What is your sister-in-law's name?
1.20 What is your niece's name?
1.21 What is your mother-in-law called?

1.27 (Her name is) Mary.
She's [She is] called Mary.

1.22 Are you an only child?

1.28 No, I have two sisters.
1.29 No, I have an older brother.
1.30 No, I have a twin sister.

1.23 What job does your father do?
1.24 What job does your mother do?

1.31 He/She works in an office.
1.32 He/She works in a factory.
1.33 He/She works in a shop.
1.34 He/She is an office worker.
1.35 He/She is a labourer.
1.36 He/She is a (primary) teacher.
1.37 He/She is unemployed.

1.12 ኣደኻ/ኺ መን ትብሃል፧
1.13 ዓባይካ/ኪ መን ትብሃል፧
1.14 ሓውትኻ/ኺ መን ትብሃል፧
1.15 ኣሞኻ/ኺ፡ ሓትኖኻ/ኺ መን ትብሃል፧
1.16 ወዲ ሓውኻ/ኺ ሓውትኻ/ኺ መን ይብሃል፧
1.17 ጓልካ መን ትብሃል፧
1.18 በዓልቲ ቤትካ መን ትብሃል፧
1.19 ሰይቲ ሓውኻ/ኺ መን ትብሃል፧
1.20 ጓል ሓወቦኻ/ኺ፡ ኣሞኻ/ኺ፡
ሓትኖኻ/ኺ፡ ኣኮኻ/ኺ፡ መን ትብሃል፧
1.21 ሓማትካ/ኪ መን ትብሃል፧
1.22 እንኮ ውላድ ዲኻ/ኺ፧

1.27 ምርያም ትብሃል

1.28 ኣይፋልን፡ ክልተ ኣሓት ኣለዋኒ
1.29 ኣይፋልን፡ ዓቢ ሓው ኣሎኒ
1.30 ኣይፋልን፡ ማንታ ሓውቲ ኣላትኒ

1.23 ኣቦኻ/ኺ እንታይ ይሰርሕ፧
1.24 ኣደኻ/ኺ እንታይ ትሰርሕ፧

1.31 ኣብ ቤት ጽሕፈት ይ/ትሰርሕ
1.32 ኣብ ፋብሪካ ይ/ትሰርሕ
1.33 ኣብ ድኳን ይ/ትሰርሕ
1.34 ሰራሕተኛ ቤትጽሕፈት ኢዩ/ያ
1.35 ሚኑዋለ ኢዩ/ያ
1.36 መምህር ኢዩ/ያ
1.37 ስራሕ የብሉን/ላን

1.12 Come si chiama tua madre?
1.13 Come si chiama tua nonna?
1.14 Come si chiama tua sorella?
1.15 Come si chiama tua zia?
1.16 Come si chiama tua cugina?
1.17 Come si chiama tua figlia?
1.18 Come si chiama tua moglie?
1.19 Come si chiama tua cognata?
1.20 Come si chiama tua nipote?
1.21 Come si chiama tua suocera?
1.22 Sei figlio unico?
Sei figlia unica?

1.27 Si chiama Maria.

1.28 No, ho due sorelle.
1.29 No, ho un fratello maggiore.
1.30 No, ho una sorella gemella.

1.23 Che lavoro fa tuo padre?
1.24 Che lavoro fa tua madre?

1.31 Lavora in un ufficio.
1.32 Lavora in una fabbrica.
1.33 Lavora in un negozio.
1.34 E' impiegato/impiegata.
1.35 E' operaio/operaia.
1.36 E' maestro/maestra.
1.37 E' disoccupato/disoccupata.

3 HOUSE AND HOME

HOW TO ...
1. **Say whether you live in a house, flat, etc., and ask others the same**
2. **Find out about garage, garden, etc.**
3. **Offer to help**
4. **Ask where places and things are in a house**
5. **Ask if another person needs soap, a towel, etc.**
6. **Invite someone to come in, to sit down**
7. **Thank someone for hospitality**

1.1 Where do you live?

1.2 I live in the town-centre.
1.3 I live in the suburbs.
1.4 I live in a flat.
1.5 I live in a block of flats.
1.6 I live in a villa.

ገዛን መንበርን

ከመይ ጌርካ ...
1. ኣብ ቪላ ወይ ኣፓርትማ ወዘተ ትቕመጥ ምኻንካ ከም እትገልጽ ከምኡ ድማ ንኻልኦት ከም እትሓትት
2. ጋራጅ ጃርዲን ወዘተ እንተ'ሎ ከም እትሓትት
3. ሓገዝ ከም እትውፊ
4. ክፍልታትን ኣቕሑን ኣበይ ከም ዝርከቡን ከም እትሓትት
5. ንሓደ ሰብ ሳምና ሹጎማኖ ወዘተ ዘድልዮ ምኻኑ ከም እትሓትት
6. ንሰብ ንኺኣቱን ኮፍ ንኺብልን ከም እትዕድም
7. ንሓደ ሰብ ብዝገበረልካ ኣቀባብላ ከም እተመስግኖ

1.1 ኣበይ ትቕመጥ/ጢ፧

1.2 ኣብ ማእከል ከተማ እቕመጥ
1.3 ካብ ከተማ ወጻኢ እቕመጥ
1.4 ኣብ ኣፓርትማ እቕመጥ
1.5 ኣብ ሓደ ርሻን እቕመጥ
1.6 ኣብ ሓንቲ ቪላ እቕመጥ

CASA

Come ...
1. **dire se si abita in una villa, in un appartamento, ecc., e chiedere lo stesso ad altri**
2. **chiedere se ci sono un garage, un giardino, ecc.**
3. **offrire il proprio aiuto**
4. **chiedere dove si trovano le stanze e gli oggetti in una casa**
5. **chiedere a qualcuno se ha bisogno del sapone, di un asciugamano, ecc.**
6. **invitare qualcuno ad entrare, ad accomodarsi**
7. **ringraziare qualcuno per l'ospitalità**

1.1 Dove abiti?

1.2 Abito in centro.
1.3 Abito in periferia.
1.4 Abito in un appartamento.
1.5 Abito in un palazzo.
1.6 Abito in una villa.

2.1 Is there a garage?
2.2 Is there a garden?
2.3 Is there central heating?
2.4 Is there a lift ?

2.5 Yes, there is.
2.6 No, there isn't.

3.1 Can I give you a hand ?
3.2 Can I be of any help?
3.3 Can I do something?
3.4 Can I lay the table ?
3.5 Can I clear the table ?
3.6 Can I wash the dishes?
3.7 Can I make something to eat?
3.8 Can I do the dusting?
3.9 Can I do the ironing?

3.10 No thank you, there is no need.
3.11 (No, leave it!) I can manage.
3.12 Yes, thank you ...

4.1 Where's [Where is] the bathroom?
4.2 Where's the toilet?
4.3 Where's the fridge?
4.4 Where's the garage?

4.5 It's opposite ...
4.6 It's at the end of ...
4.7 It's next to ...
4.8 It's in front of ...

2.1 ጋራጅ ኣለዎዶ፧
2.2 ጃርዲን ኣለዎዶ፧
2.3 መውዓይ ማይ ኣለዎዶ፧
2.4 ሊፍት ኣለዎዶ፧
2.5 እወ፡ ኣሎዎ
2.6 ኣይፋልን፡ የብሉን

3.1 ክሕግዘካዶ/ ክሕግዘኪዶ፧
3.2 ክተሓጋገዘዶ፧
3.3 ገለ ነገር ክገብርዶ፧
3.4 መኣዲ ክቐርብዶ፧
3.5 ነዚ መኣዲ ክልዕሎዶ፧
3.6 ኣቕሑ ክሓጽብዶ፧
3.7 ዝብላዕ ክቐርብዶ፧
3.8 ነዚ ገዛይ ክነጋግፎዶ፧
3.9 ክስታርርዶ፧
3.10 ደሓን፡ የቐንየለይ፡ ኣየድልን ኢዩ
3.11 ግደፎ ድሓን ባዕለይ ክገብሮ እየ/
ግደፊዮ ድሓን ባዕለይ ክገብሮ እየ
3.12 ሕራይ፡ የቐንየለይ

4.1 መሕጸብ ነብሲ ኣበይ ኢዩ፧
4.2 ሽቓቕ ኣበይ ኢዩ፧
4.3 ፍሪጅ ኣበይ ኣሎ፧
4.4 ጋራጅ ኣበይ ኢዩ፧
4.5 ኣብ ፊት ናይ ...
4.6 ኣብ ጫፍ ናይ ...
4.7 ኣብ ጐድኒ ናይ ...
4.8 ኣብ ቅድሚ ናይ ...

2.1 C'è il garage?
2.2 C'è il giardino?
2.3 C'è il riscaldamento centrale?
2.4 C'è l'ascensore?
2.5 Sì, c'è.
2.6 No, non c'è.

3.1 Posso darti una mano ?
3.2 Posso esserti utile?
3.3 Posso fare qualcosa?
3.4 Posso apparecchiare?
3.5 Posso sparecchiare?
3.6 Posso lavare i piatti?
3.7 Posso preparare da mangiare?
3.8 Posso spolverare?
3.9 Posso stirare?
3.10 No, grazie! Non c'è bisogno.
3.11 (No, lascia stare!) Faccio da solo/a.
3.12 Sì, grazie...

4.1 Dov'è il bagno?
4.2 Dov'è il gabinetto?
4.3 Dov'è il frigorifero?
4.4 Dov'è il garage?
4.5 E' davanti a...
4.6 E' in fondo a...
4.7 E' accanto a...
4.8 E' di fronte a...

5.1 Where's the pillow?
5.2 Where's the blanket?
5.3 Where's the cutlery?
5.4 Where are the plates?

5.5 Here it is.
5.6 Here it is.
5.7 Here they are.
5.8 Here they are.

6.1 Do you need any soap?
6.2 Do you need any toothpaste?
6.3 Do you need a towel?
6.4 Do you need an alarm clock?
6.5 Do you need anything?

6.6 Yes, I need some ...
6.7 Yes, I need a ...

7.1 May I come in?
7.2 May I?
7.3 Am I interrupting?

7.4 Come in!
7.5 Make yourself comfortable!
7.6 Not at all/(Please) come in!

8.1 Thank you for your hospitality!
8.2 You have (all) been so kind!
8.3 I hope I can do the same for you soon!

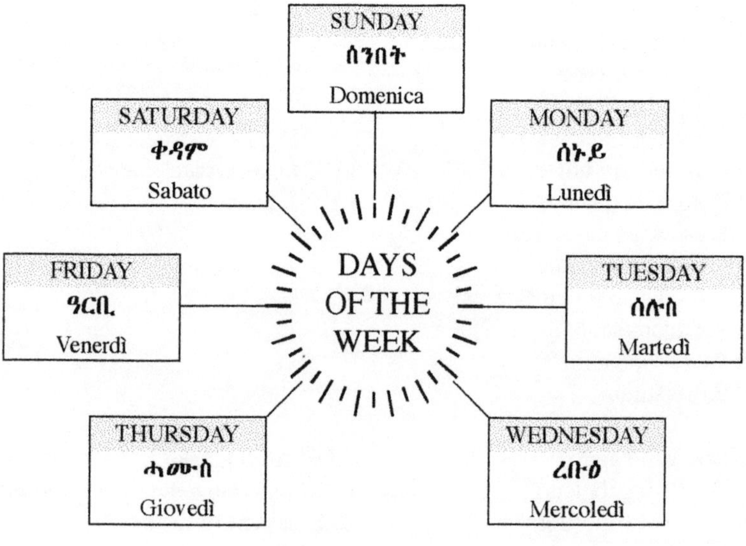

5.1 መተርኣስ ኣበይ ኣሎ፧
5.2 ኮቦርታ ኣበይ ኣሎ፧
5.3 ማንካታትን ካራን ኣበይ ኣሎ፧
5.4 ሽሓኒታት ኣበይ ኣሎ፧

5.5 እነሀ
5.6 እነሀ
5.7 እነሀ
5.8 እነሀ

6.1 ሳሙና የድልየካ/ኪ ዲዩ፧
6.2 መሕጸቢ ስኒ የድልየካ/ኪ ዲዩ፧
6.3 ሽጎማኖ የድልየካ/ኪ ዲዩ፧
6.4 መበራበሪ ሰዓት የድልየካ/ኪ ዲዩ፧
6.5 ዘድልየካ/ኪ ነገር ኣሎ ዲዩ፧

6.6 እወ ... መድልየኒ ነይሩ
6.7 እወ ... ምደለኹ

7.1 ክኣቱዶ፧
7.2 ፍቓድ ዲዩ፧
7.3 ረቢሸ ዲየ፧

7.4 እቶ/ እተዊ
7.5 ኮፍ በል/ሊ
7.6 እተዉ/ እተዋ

8.1 ብዝተገብረለይ ኣቀባብላ ኣመስግን
8.2 ብሓቂ ምስጋና ዝግባኣኩም
ኢ.ኹም
8.3 ኣብ ካሕሳኹም የውዕለና

5.1 Dove è il cuscino ?
5.2 Dove è la coperta?
5.3 Dove sono le posate?
5.4 Dove sono i piatti?

5.5 Eccolo.
5.6 Eccola.
5.7 Eccole.
5.8 Eccoli.

6.1 Hai bisogno del sapone ?
6.2 Hai bisogno del dentifricio?
6.3 Hai bisogno dell'asciugamano?
6.4 Hai bisogno della sveglia?
6.5 Hai bisogno di qualcosa ?

6.6 Sì, avrei bisogno di ...
6.7 Sì, mi servirebbe ...

7.1 Posso entrare?
7.2 Permesso?
7.3 Disturbo?

7.4 Avanti!
7.5 Accomodati!
7.6 (Prego), entra!

8.1 Grazie per l'ospitalità!
8.2 Siete stati molto gentili!
8.3 Spero di poter ricambiare presto!

DAILY ROUTINE

HOW TO ...
1. State at what time you usually get up, go to bed and have meals
2. Say whether you have a job. If so, what job, what working hours, how much you earn

1.1 What time do you wake up?	1.14 I wake up at ...
1.2 What time do you get up?	1.15 I get up at ...
1.3 What time do you have breakfast?	1.16 I have breakfast at ...
1.4 What time do you have lunch?	1.17 I have lunch at ...
1.5 What time do you have dinner?	1.18 I have dinner at ...
1.6 What time do you go to bed?	1.19 I go to bed at ...
1.7 What time do (you go to) sleep?	1.20 I (go to) sleep at ...

መዓልታዊ ልማድ

ከመይ ጌርካ ...
1. በየናይ ሰዓት ከም ዚትንሳእ ከም ዚድቀስ ከም ዚብላዕ ከም እትገልጽ
2. ስራሕ ምህላውካን እንታይ ዓይነት ስራሕ ምዃኑን ክንደይ ሰዓት ከም እትሰርሕን ክንደይ ከም እትኽፈልን ከም እትገልጽ

1.1 ሰዓት ክንደይ ትበራበር/ሪ፧
1.2 ሰዓት ክንደይ ትትንስእ/ኢ፧
1.3 ሰዓት ክንደይ ትቑርስ/ሲ፧
1.4 ሰዓት ክንደይ ትምሳሕ/ስሒ፧
1.5 ሰዓት ክንደይ ትድረር/ሪ፧
1.6 ሰዓት ክንደይ ኣብ ዓራት ትኣቱ/ትዊ፧
1.7 ሰዓት ክንደይ ትድቅስ/ሲ፧

1.14 ሰዓት ... እበራበር
1.15 ሰዓት ... እትንስእ
1.16 ሰዓት ... እቑርስ
1.17 ሰዓት ... እምሳሕ
1.18 ሰዓት ... እድረር
1.19 ሰዓት ... ኣብ ዓራት እኣቱ
1.20 ሰዓት ... እድቅስ

ABITUDINI GIORNALIERE

Come ...
1. dire a che ora di solito ci si alza, si va a dormire e si mangia
2. dire se si ha un lavoro, di che lavoro si tratta, quante ore si lavora, quanto si guadagna

1.1 A che ora ti svegli?
1.2 A che ora ti alzi?
1.3 A che ora fai colazione ?
1.4 A che ora pranzi?
1.5 A che ora ceni?
1.6 A che ora vai a letto ?
1.7 A che ora vai a dormire ?

1.14 Mi sveglio alle ...
1.15 Mi alzo alle ...
1.16 Faccio colazione alle ...
1.17 Pranzo alle ...
1.18 Ceno alle ...
1.19 Vado a letto alle ...
1.20 Vado a dormire alle ...

1.8 Have you found a job?

1.9 Is it tiring?
1.10 Is it demanding?

1.11 How many hours do you work?

1.12 How much do you earn?
1.13 Do you earn a lot?

1.21 Yes, I work in a bar.
1.22 I give English lessons.

1.23 No, not really.
1.24 Yes, but I like it.

1.25 I work 8 hours a day.

1.26 I earn ... an hour.
1.27 I earn ... a month.

1.8 ስራሕ ረኺብካ/ኪ ዶ፧

1.9 ኣድካሚ ዲዩ፧
1.10 በዳሂ ዲዩ፧

1.11 ክንደይ ሰዓት ትሰርሕ/ሒ፧

1.12 ክንደይ ትኸፈል/ሊ፧
1.13 ብዙሕዶ ትኸፈል/ሊ፧

1.21 እወ፡ ኣብ ሓደ ባር እሰርሕ ኣለኹ
1.22 ቋንቋ እንግሊዝ እምህር ኣለኹ

1.23 ብዙሕ ኣይኮነን
1.24 እወ፡ ግን እፈትዎ እየ

1.25 ንመዓልቲ 8 ሰዓት እሰርሕ

1.26 ንሰዓት ... ብር እኽፈል
1.27 ንወርሒ ... ብር እኽፈል

1.8 Hai trovato un lavoro?

1.9 E' faticoso?
1.10 E' impegnativo?

1.11 Quante ore lavori?

1.12 Quanto guadagni?
1.13 Guadagni molto?

1.21 Sì, lavoro in un bar.
1.22 Do lezioni di inglese.

1.23 No, non molto.
1.24 Sì, ma mi piace.

1.25 Lavoro 8 ore al giorno.

1.26 Guadagno ... lire all'ora.
1.27 Guadagno ... lire al mese.

How to describe your house, flat, etc.
ከመይ ጌርካ ነቲ እትነብረሉ ቦታ ከም እትገልጽ
Come descrivere la propria abitazione ...

Key Words	ቀንዲ ቃላት	Parole chiave
there is, there are	ኣላ/ኣሎ ኣለዉ/ኣለዋ	c'è, ci sono
on the right	ንየማን	a destra
on the left	ንጸጋም	a sinistra
up	ላዕሊ	in alto
down	ታሕቲ	in basso
in the middle of	ኣብ መንጎ ናይ	in mezzo a
at the bottom of	ኣብ ትሕቲ ናይ	in fondo a
on top of	ኣብ ልዕሊ ናይ	in cima a
above	ልዕሊ	sopra
below	ትሕቲ	sotto
near	ጥቓ	vicino a
next to	ጐኒ	accanto a
opposite/in front of	ፊት	di fronte a
inside	ኣብ ውሽጢ	dentro
around	ከባቢ	intorno

Vocabulary	መዝገበ ቃላት	Vocabolario
1 lift	1 ሊፍት	1 l'ascensore
2 bathroom	2 ባኞ	2 il bagno
3 balcony	3 ገበላ	3 il balcone
4 bedroom	4 ክፍሊ መደቀሲ	4 la camera da letto
5 cellar	5 መኻዚኖ	5 la cantina
6 corridor	6 ኮሪደዮ	6 il corridoio
7 kitchen	7 ክሽነ	7 la cucina
8 entrance hall	8 ኣፍደገ	8 l'entrata
9 window	9 መስኮት	9 la finestra
10 wall	10 መንደቕ	10 la parete
11 floor	11 ባይታ	11 il pavimento
12 door	12 ማዕጾ	12 la porta
13 main door	13 ኣፍ ደገ	13 il portone
14 first/second floor	14 ቀዳማይ/ካልኣይ ደርቢ	14 il primo/secondo piano
15 dining-room	15 ቤት መኣዲ	15 la sala da pranzo
16 stairs	16 መሳልል / ኣስካላ	16 le scale
17 roof	17 ናሕሲ	17 il tetto

4 GEOGRAPHICAL SURROUNDINGS

HOW TO ...
1. Give information about your home town or village and surrounding area
2. Describe the weather conditions (see p. 128)
3. Describe the climate of your own country and enquire about the climate in another country (see p. 128)

1.1 Where do you live?

1.22 I live in Eritrea.
1.23 I live in Italy.
1.24 I live in England.
1.25 I live in Rome.
1.26 I live in London.
1.27 I live in Chicago.

ጀዮግራፍያዊ ኣቀማምጣን ኩነታት ኣየርን

ከመር ጌርካ ...
1. ብዛዕባ ከተማኻን ዓድኻን ወይ ከኣ ከባቢኻ ሓበሬታ ክም እትህብ

1.1 ኣበይ ትነብር/ ኣበይ ትነብሪ፧

1.22 ኣብ ኤርትራ እቕመጥ
1.23 ኣብ ዓዲ ጣልያን እቕመጥ
1.24 ኣብ ዓዲ እንግሊዝ እቕመጥ
1.24 ኣብ ሮማ እቕመጥ
1.26 ኣብ ለንደን እቕመጥ
1.27 ኣብ ሺካጎ እቕመጥ

AMBIENTE GEOGRAFICO

Come ...
1. dare informazioni sulla propria città o villaggio e sulla zona circostante
2. descrivere le condizioni meteorologiche (vedi p. 129)
3. descrivere il clima del proprio paese e porre domande su quello di un altro paese (vedi p. 129)

1.1 Dove vivi?

1.22 Vivo in Eritrea.
1.23 Vivo in Italia.
1.24 Vivo in Inghilterra.
1.25 Vivo a Roma.
1.26 Vivo a Londra.
1.27 Vivo a Chicago.

1.2 Where are you from?	1.28 I'm [I am] from Massawa. 1.29 I'm from Turin.
1.3 Where is it?	1.30 It's [It is] in northern Italy. 1.31 It's in central Italy. 1.32 It's in southern Italy. 1.33 It's in the north of Italy. 1.34 It's in the south of Italy.
1.4 Is it a large city?	1.35 No, it is a village in the mountains. 1.36 No, it is a village on a hill. 1.37 No, it is a village by the sea. 1.38 No, it is a village on a river. 1.39 No, it is a village on a lake.
1.5 Which is the nearest city?	1.40 (It's near) Turin. 1.41 (It's near) Naples. 1.42 (It's near) Asmara.

1.2 ወዲ ኣየናይ ከባቢ ኢኻ/ ጓል ኣየናይ ከባቢ ኢኺ፧

1.28 ወዲ/ጓል ባጽዕ እየ
1.29 ወዲ/ጓል ቶሪኖ እየ

1.3 ኣበይ ይርከብ/ትርከብ፧

1.30 ኣብ ሰሜናዊ ዓዲ ጥልያን ይርከብ/ ትርከብ
1.31 ኣብ ማእከል ዓዲ ጥልያን ይርከብ/ ትርከብ
1.32 ኣብ ደቡባዊ ዓዲ ጥልያን ይርከብ/ ትርከብ
1.33 ኣብ ሰሜን ዓዲ ጥልያን ይርከብ/ ትርከብ
1.34 ኣብ ደቡብ ዓዲ ጥልያን ይርከብ/ ትርከብ

1.4 ሓንቲ ዓባይ ከተማ ዲያ፧

1.35 ኣብ ዝባን እትርከብ ንእሽቶ ዓዲ ኢያ
1.36 ኣይፋልን፡ ኣብ እምባ እተደኮነት ንእሽቶ ዓዲ ኢያ
1.37 ኣብ ጥቓ ባሕሪ እትርከብ ንእሽቶ ዓዲ ኢያ
1.38 ኣብ ጥቓ ወሓዚ እትርከብ ንእሽቶ ዓዲ ኢያ
1.39 ኣብ ጥቓ ቀላይ እትርከብ ንእሽቶ ዓዲ ኢያ

1.5 እታ ዝቐረበት ከተማ ኣየናይቲ ኢያ፧

1.40 (ጥቓ) ቶሪኖ ኢያ
1.41 (ጥቓ) ናፖሊ ኢያ
1.42 (ጥቓ) ኣስመራ ኢያ

1.2 Di dove sei?

1.28 Sono di Massaua.
1.29 Sono di Torino.

1.3 Dove si trova?

1.30 Si trova nell'Italia settentrionale.
1.31 Si trova nell'Italia centrale.
1.32 Si trova nell'Italia meridionale.
1.33 Si trova nel nord Italia.
1.34 Si trova nel sud Italia.

1.4 E' una grande città?

1.35 No, è un villaggio in montagna.
1.36 No, è un piccolo paese in collina.
1.37 No, è un piccolo paese sul mare.
1.38 No, è un piccolo paese su un fiume.
1.39 No, è un piccolo paese su un lago.

1.5 Qual è la città più vicina?

1.40 (E' vicino/a a) Torino.
1.41 (E' vicino/a a) Napoli.
1.42 (E' vicino/a ad) Asmara.

1.6 What's the country-side like?	1.43 It's hilly. 1.44 It's enchanting. 1.45 It's monotonous. 1.46 It's picturesque. 1.47 It's wonderful.
1.7 Where do you live?	1.48 I live in the old part of town. 1.49 I live in the suburbs.
1.8 Is there an airport? 1.9 Is there a sports centre? 1.10 Is there a shopping centre? 1.11 Is there a castle? 1.12 Is there a cathedral?	1.50 Yes, there is ... 1.51 No, there isn't ...

1.6 እቲ ከባቢ ዓዲ ከመይ ይመስል፧

1.43 ብጎቦ እተኸበበ ኢዩ
1.44 ማራኺ ኢዩ
1.45 ኣሰልቻዊ ኢዩ
1.46 ኣደናቒ ኢዩ
1.47 ኣደንጻዊ ኢዩ

1.7 ኣበይ ትነብር / ትነብሪ፧

1.48 ኣብቲ ናይ ቀደም ከተማ እነብር
1.49 ኣብ ከባቢ እቕመጥ

1.8 መዕረፍ ነፈርቲ ኣሎዶ፧
1.9 ናይ ስፖርት ማእከል ኣሎዶ፧
1.10 ንድኳን ዝኸውን ማእከል ኣሎዶ፧
1.11 ካስተሎ ኣሎዶ፧
1.12 ቤተ ክርስትያን ኣሎዶ፧

1.50 እወ፡ ... ኣሎ
1.51 ... የሎን

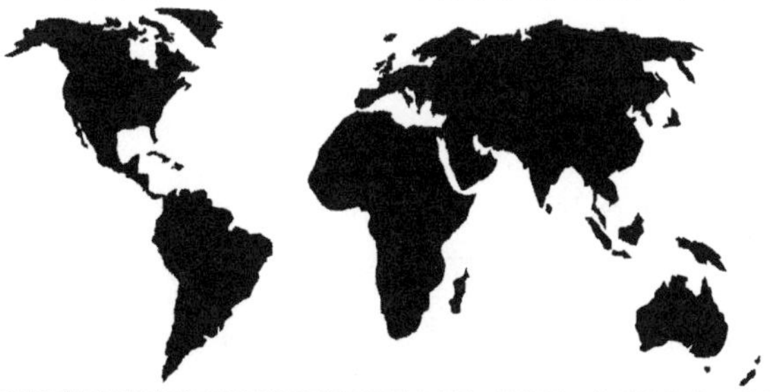

1.6 Com'è il paesaggio?

1.43 E' collinare.
1.44 E' incantevole.
1.45 E' monotono.
1.46 E' pittoresco.
1.47 E' stupendo.

1.7 Dove abiti?

1.48 Abito nel centro storico.
1.49 Abito in periferia.

1.8 C'è un aeroporto?
1.9 C'è un centro sportivo?
1.10 C'è un centro commerciale?
1.11 C'è un castello?
1.12 C'è una cattedrale?

1.50 Sì, c'è ...
1.51 No, non c'è ...

1.13 Are there many monuments?
1.14 Are there many shops?
1.15 Are there many gardens?
1.16 Are there many theatres?
1.17 Are there many avenues?
1.18 Are there many discotheques?
1.19 Are there many fountains?
1.20 Are there many industries?
1.21 Are there many factories?

1.52 Yes, there are...
1.53 No, there aren't...

1.13 ብዙሕ ሓወልትታት ኣለዉ፧
1.14 ብዙሕ ድኳናት ኣለዉ፧
1.15 ብዙሕ ጀራዲን ኣለዉ፧
1.16 ብዙሕ ትያትራት ኣለዉ፧
1.17 ብዙሕ መገድታት ኣለዉ፧
1.18 ብዙሕ ዲስኮተክ ኣለዉ፧
1.19 ብዙሕ ፈልፋሊ ማያት ኣለዉ፧
1.20 ብዙሕ ኢንዱስትሪታት ኣለዉ፧
1.21 ብዙሕ ፋብሪካታት ኣለዉ፧

1.52 እወ፡ ... ኣሎ
1.53 ኣይፋልን፡ ... የለን

1.13 Ci sono molti monumenti?
1.14 Ci sono molti negozi?
1.15 Ci sono molti giardini?
1.16 Ci sono molti teatri?
1.17 Ci sono molti viali?
1.18 Ci sono molte discoteche?
1.19 Ci sono molte fontane?
1.20 Ci sono molte industrie?
1.21 Ci sono molte fabbriche?

1.52 Sì, ci sono ...
1.53 No, non ci sono ...

INFORMALE (tu)	**FORMALE (Lei)**
Di dove sei?	Di dov'è?
Dov'è la tua scuola?	Dov'è la sua scuola?
Che cosa fai di solito il week end?	Che cosa fa di solito il week end?
Ti piace vivere in Gran Bretagna?	Le piace vivere in Gran Bretagna?
Ti piacerebbe vivere in Italia?	Le piacerebbe vivere in Italia?

United Kingdom (Great Britain and Northern Ireland)

Borders:	The Atlantic Ocean, the North Sea, the English Channel
Area:	244,761 square km.
Population:	58,422,000
Density:	238 inhabitants per square km
Language:	English
Monetary Unit:	Pound Sterling
Capital:	London (6,904,600 inhabitants)
Flag:	The flag's colours are blue, white and red

Eritrea

Borders:	Sudan, Ethiopia, Red Sea, Djibouti
Area:	Approximately 124,300 square km.
Population:	Approximately 3,779,000
Density:	32 inhabitants per square km
Language:	Tigrinya, Arabic (English and Italian are widely spoken)
Monetary Unit:	Nakfa
Capital:	Asmara (approximately 400,000 inhabitants)
Flag:	The flag's colours are green, red, blue and yellow

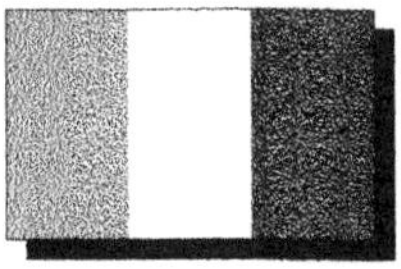

Italy

Borders:	France, Switzerland, Austria and Slovenia
Area:	301,277 square km.
Population:	57,313,000
Density:	190 inhabitants per square km
Language:	Italian
Monetary Unit:	Italian Lira
Capital:	Rome (2,773,889 inhabitants)
Flag:	The flag's colours are green, white and red

5 TRAVEL AND TRANSPORT

HOW TO ...
1. Say how you get to school or place of work
2. Attract the attention of a passer-by
3. Ask the way to a place
4. Ask if there is a place nearby
5. Say you do not understand
6. Ask someone to repeat what they have said
7. Thank someone

1.1 How do you get to school?
1.2 How do you get to work?

1.3 By bus.
1.4 By car.
1.5 By train.
1.6 By bicycle.
1.7 By coach.
1.8 On foot.

መጎዓዝያ

ከመይ ጌርካ ...
1. ናብ ቤትትምህርቲ ወይ ናብ ስራሕ ከም እትኸይድ ምግላጽ
2. ኣቓልቦ ኣጋር ከም እትስሕብ
3. ናብ ሓደ ውሱን ቦታ ንምብጻሕ ከም እትሓትት
4. ቅርበት ቦታ ከም እትሓትት
5. ኣይተረደኣንን ከም እትብል
6. ነቲ እተባህለ ድገሙለይ ከም እትብል
7. ከም እተመስግን

1.1 ብኸመይ ናብ ቤት ትምህርቲ ትኸይድ፧
1.2 ብኸመይ ናብ ስራሕ ትኸይድ፧

1.3 ብኣውቶቡስ
1.4 ብመኪና
1.5 ብባቡር
1.6 ብቢችክለታ
1.7 ብኣውቶቡስ
1.8 ብእግሪ

TRASPORTI

Come ...
1. dire con quali mezzi si raggiunge la scuola o il posto di lavoro
2. attirare l'attenzione di un passante
3. chiedere informazioni per raggiungere un determinato luogo
4. chiedere se un determinato luogo è vicino
5. dire che non si è capito
6. chiedere a qualcuno di ripetere

1.1 Come vai a scuola?
1.2 Come vai al lavoro?

1.3 In autobus.
1.4 In macchina.
1.5 In treno.
1.6 In bicicletta.
1.7 In corriera.
1.8 A piedi.

1.9 How long does it take?

1.10 (About) 10 minutes.
1.11 (About) an hour ...

2.1 Excuse me!

2.2 Yes!

3.1 Where's [Where is] the museum?
3.2 Where's the castle?
3.3 Where's the post office?
3.4 Where's the information centre?
3.5 Where's the church ?
3.6 Where's the chemist?
3.7 Where's the swimming pool?
3.8 Can you tell me the way to the police station?
3.9 Can you tell me the way to the bus stop?
3.10 Can you tell me the way to the station?

3.11 Take the first on the right.
3.12 Take the second on the right.
3.13 Take the third on the right.
3.14 Turn left.
3.15 (Go) straight on.
3.16 Go as far as the traffic lights.
3.17 Go as far as the cross-road.
3.18 Cross the road.
3.19 Cross the pedestrian crossing.
3.20 It's there, on your right.

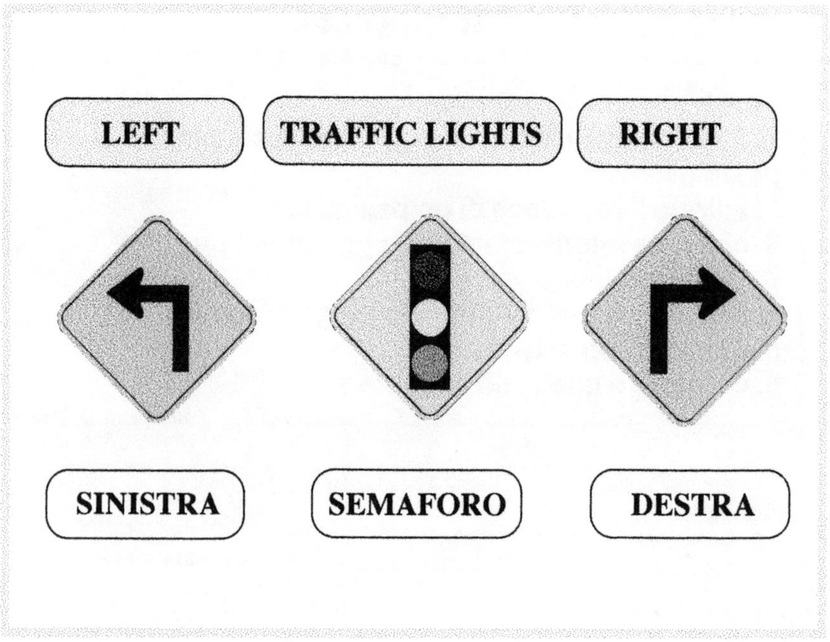

1.9 ክንደይ (ሰዓት) ይወስድ፧

1.10 ዳርጋ 10 ደቓይቕ
1.11 ዳርጋ 1 ሰዓት

2.1 ይቕረታ

2.2 እሺ፡ እንታይ ነይሩ

3.1 ቤተ መዘክር ኣበይ ከ ምዝኾነ (ዚርከብ) ምሓበርካኒዶ፧
3.2 ካስቴሎ ኣበይ ከም ዝኾነ (ዚርከብ) ምሓበርካኒዶ፧
3.3 ቤት ፖስታ ኣበይ ከም ዝኾነ (ዚርከብ) ምሓበርካኒዶ፧
3.4 ቤት ጽሕፈት ዜና ኣበይ ከም ዝኾነ (ዚርከብ) ምሓበርካኒዶ፧
3.5 ቤትክርስትያን ኣበይ ከም ዝኾነ (ዚርከብ) ምሓበርካኒዶ፧
3.6 ቤት መድሃኒት ኣበይ ከም ዝኾነ (ዚርከብ) ምሓበርካኒዶ፧
3.7 መሐንበሲ ኣበይ ከም ዝኾነ (ዚርከብ) ምሓበርካኒዶ፧
3.8 እንዳ ፖሊስ ኣበይ ከም ዝኾነ (ዚርከብ) ምሓበርካኒዶ፧
3.9 መዕረፍ ኣውቶቡስ ኣበይ ከም ዝኾነ (ዚርከብ) ምሓበርካኒዶ፧
3.10 መዕረፍ ባቡራት ኣበይ ከም ዝኾነ (ዚርከብ) ምሓበርካኒዶ፧

3.11 ኣብታ ቀዳመይቲ ኣንጎሎ ንየማን ተጠወ
3.12 ኣብታ ካልአይቲ ኣንጎሎ ንየማን ተጠወ
3.13 ኣብታ ሳልሰይቲ ኣንጎሎ ንየማን ተጠወ
3.14 ንጸጋም ተኣለ
3.15 ንቕድሚት ቀጽል
3.16 ክሳብ ሰማፎሮ ቀጽል
3.17 ክሳብ ቀራና መገዲ ቀጽል
3.18 ጽርግያ ተሳገር
3.19 በቲ ጻዕዳ መስመር ተሳገር
3.20 ኣብኡ 'ዩ፡ ብየማንካ

1.9 Quanto ci metti? / Quanto impieghi?

1.10 (Circa) 10 minuti.
1.11 (Circa) un'ora.

2.1 (Senta), scusi!

2.2 Sì, (dica)!

3.1 (Mi sa dire) dov'è il museo?
3.2 (Mi sa dire) dov'è il castello?
3.3 (Mi sa dire) dov'è l'ufficio postale?
3.4 (Mi sa dire) dov'è l'ufficio informazioni?
3.5 (Mi sa dire) dov'è la chiesa?
3.6 (Mi sa dire) dov'è la farmacia?
3.7 (Mi sa dire) dov'è la piscina?
3.8 (Mi sa dire) dov'è la questura?
3.9 (Mi sa dire) dov'è la fermata dell'autobus?
3.10 (Mi sa dire) dov'è la stazione?

3.11 Prenda la prima a destra.
3.12 Prenda la seconda a destra.
3.13 Prenda la terza a destra.
3.14 Volti a sinistra.
3.15 Continui (sempre) dritto.
3.16 Vada fino al semaforo.
3.17 Vada fino all'incrocio.
3.18 Attraversi la strada.
3.19 Attraversi il passaggio pedonale.
3.20 E' lì, sulla destra.

4.1 Excuse me, is there a bank near here?
4.2 Excuse me, is there a restaurant near here?

4.4 20 metres, on the left.
4.5 Opposite...
4.6 Next to...
4.7 Near...
4.8 On the road parallel to this one.

4.3 Is it very far from here?

4.9 No, (it's about) ten minutes walk.
4.10 Yes, you'll have to take a taxi.

5.1 Excuse me, what did you say?
5.2 I don't understand.

6.1 Could you say it again, please?
6.2 Could you speak more slowly, please?

7.1 Thank you!
7.2 Thank you very much!
7.3 Very kind of you!

4.1 ይቕረታ፡ ኣብዚ ከባቢ ባንክ ኣሎዶ፧
4.2 ይቕረታ፡ ኣብዚ ቀረባ ቤት መግቢ ኣሎዶ፧

4.4 20 ሜትሮ ንጸጋም
4.5 ብመንጽር ...
4.6 ጥቓ፡ ኣብ ጐድኒ ...
4.7 ጥቓ ...
4.8 ማዕረ'ዚ መገዲ/ ብመንጽር'ዚ መገዲ

4.3 ካብዚ ኣዚዩ ርሑቕ ዲዩ፧

4.9 ኣይኮነን፡ ብእግሪ ዳርጋ 10 ደቒቕ ይወስድ
4.10 እወ፡ ታክሲ ምውሳድ ከድልየካ ኢዩ

5.1 ይቕረታ፡ እንታይ'ዩ ዝበልካ፧
5.2 ኣይተረደኣንን

6.1 ክትደግሙለይ ምኽኣልኩምዶ፧
6.2 ቀስ ኢልኩም ክትዛረቡ ምኽኣልኩምዶ፧

7.1 የቐንየለይ
7.2 ብዙሕ የቐንየለይ
7.3 ብዙሕ ተሓጒሰ

4.1 Scusi, c'è una banca qui vicino ?
4.2 Scusi, c'è un ristorante qui vicino ?

4.4 A 20 metri, sulla sinistra.
4.5 Di fronte a ...
4.6 Accanto a ...
4.7 Vicino a ...
4.8 Nella via parallela a questa.

4.3 E' molto lontano da qui?

4.9 No, (circa) 10 minuti a piedi.
4.10 Sì, deve prendere un taxi.

5.1 Come, scusi?
5.2 Non capisco.

6.1 Può ripetere, per favore?
6.2 Può parlare più piano, per favore?

7.1 Grazie!
7.2 Mille grazie!
7.3 E' molto gentile!

TRAVEL BY PUBLIC TRANSPORT

HOW TO ...

1. Ask if there is a bus, train or coach to a particular place
2. Buy tickets specifying: single or return and class
3. Ask about the times of departure and arrival
4. Ask and check whether it is: the right platform, bus, coach or stop
5. Reserve a seat
6. Ask the time

1.1 Is there a coach to Florence?
1.2 Is there a bus to the station?

1.3 Is there an express train for Bologna?

1.4 I'm [I am] sorry, I don't know.
1.5 (Yes,) number 20.

1.6 Yes, there's [There is] one in half an hour.
1.7 Yes, there's one at ten past seven.

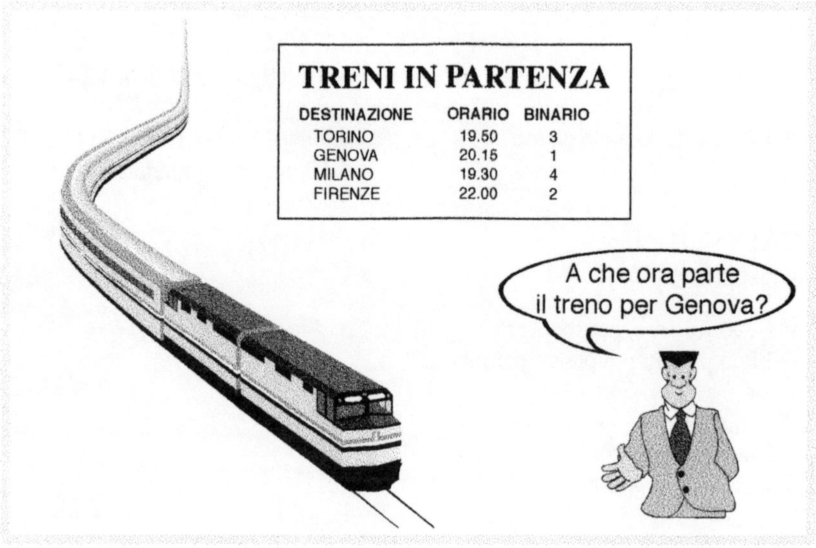
TRENI IN PARTENZA
DESTINAZIONE ORARIO BINARIO
TORINO 19.50 3
GENOVA 20.15 1
MILANO 19.30 4
FIRENZE 22.00 2
A che ora parte il treno per Genova?

ጕዕዞን መጕዓዝያን

ከመይ ጌርካ ...
1. ናብ ሓደ እተወሰነ ቦታ ዚኸዳ ኣውቶቡሳት ወይ ባቡራት እንተሃለዋ ትሓትት
2. መኸድን መምለስን ቲከት ፈሊኻ ትገዝእ
3. ናይ ምንቃልን ምምጻእን ሰዓታት ትሓትት
4. መገዲ ባቡር፡ ኣውቶቡስ፡ ደው መበሊ ልክዕ ምዃኑ ተረጋግጽ
5. ኣቐዲምካ ቦታ ትሕዝ (ትምዝገብ)
6. ሰዓት ትሓትት

1.1 ንፊረንሰ እትኸይድ ኣውቶቡስ ኣላዶ፧
1.2 ናብ መዓርፎ ባቡር እትኸይድ ኣውቶቡስ ኣላዶ፧
1.3 ንቦሎኛ እትኸይድ ቅልጥፍቲ ባቡር ኣላዶ፧

1.4 ይቕረታ፡ ኣይፈለጥኩን
1.5 እወ፡ ቍጽሪ 20
1.6 እወ፡ ድሕሪ ፍርቂ ሰዓት እትመጽእ ኣላ
1.7 እወ፡ ሰዓት ሸውዓተን ዓሰርተን እትመጽእ ኣላ

TRASPORTO PUBBLICO

Come ...
1. chiedere se c'è un autobus, un treno o una corriera per un determinato luogo
2. comprare biglietti specificando se di sola andata o di andata e ritorno e la classe
3. chiedere gli orari di partenza e di arrivo
4. chiedere e verificare se il binario, l'autobus, la corriera o la fermata sono quelli giusti
5. prenotare un posto
6. chiedere l'ora

1.1 C'è una corriera per Firenze?
1.2 C'è un autobus per la stazione?
1.3 C'è un treno espresso per Bologna?

1.4 Mi dispiace, non lo so.
1.5 Sì, il numero 20.
1.6 Sì, ce n'è uno tra mezz'ora.
1.7 Sì, ce n'è uno alle sette e dieci.

2.1 I'd like a single ticket.
2.2 I'd like a return ticket.

2.3 First class?
2.4 Second class?

3.1 What time is the next train for Rome?
3.2 What time is the next coach for Rome?

3.5 It leaves at 4.30 p.m.

3.3 What time does it leave Naples?
3.4 What time does it get to London?

3.6 It leaves at 3.00 p.m.
3.7 It gets in at 3.00 p.m.

4.1 Excuse me, is this platform 3?
4.2 Excuse me, is this the coach for ...?
4.3 Excuse me, is this the stop for ...?

4.5 Yes.
4.6 No, it's that one over there.

4.4 Which platform does the train for Genoa leave from?

4.7 It leaves from platform 3.

5.1 I'd like to reserve a seat.
5.2 I'd like to reserve a couchette.

2.1 መኸዲ ቲኬት ምሃብካኒዶ፧
2.2 መምለሲ ቲኬት ምሃብካኒዶ፧
2.3 ቀዳማይ መዓርግ፧
2.4 ካልኣይ መዓርግ፧

3.1 እታ ባቡር ሰዓት ክንደይ ኢ.ያ ናብ ሮማ እትኸይድ፧
3.2 እታ ኣውቶቡስ በየናይ ሰዓት ኢ.ያ ናብ ሮማ እትኸይድ፧
3.5 ሰዓት 4:30 ኢ.ያ እትነቅል

3.3 ሰዓት ክንደይ ኢ.ያ ካብ ናፖሊ እትነቅል፧
3.4 ሰዓት ክንደይ ኢ.ያ ናብ ሎንደን እትበጽሕ፧
3.6 ሰዓት 3 ኢ.ያ እትነቅል
3.7 ሰዓት 3 ኢ.ያ እትበጽሕ

4.1 ይቕረታ፣ እቲ መድረኽ ቍ. 3 ዲዩ፧
4.2 ይቕረታ፣ እዚ ናይ ... ኣውቶቡስ ዲዩ፧
4.3 ይቕረታ፣ ኣብዚ ዲ.ያ ... ደው እትብል፧
4.5 እወ
4.6 ኣይፋልን፣ ኣብቲኣ ኢ.ያ

4.4 እታ ናይ ጀኖቫ ባቡር ካበየናይ መድረኽ ኢ.ያ እትነቅል፧
4.7 ካብ መድረኽ ቍ.3 ኢ.ያ እትነቅል

5.1 ኮፍ መበሊ (መንበር) ኣቐዲመ ክሕዝ ምደለኹ
5.2 መደቀሲ ዓራት ኣቐዲመ ክሕዝ ምደለኹ

2.1 Vorrei un biglietto di andata.
2.2 Vorrei un biglietto di andata e ritorno.
2.3 Di prima classe?
2.4 Di seconda classe?

3.1 A che ora parte il treno per Roma?
3.2 A che ora parte la corriera per Roma?
3.5 Parte alle 16.30.

3.3A che ora parte da Napoli?
3.4 Quando arriva a Londra?
3.6 Parte alle 15.00.
3.7 Arriva alle 15.00.

4.1 Scusi, è il binario n. 3?
4.2 Scusi, è la corriera per ...?
4.3 Scusi, è la fermata per ... ?
4.5 Sì!
4.6 No, è quella (laggiù).

4.4 Da che binario parte il treno per Genova?
4.7 Parte dal binario numero 3.

5.1 Vorrei prenotare un posto.
5.2 Vorrei prenotare una cuccetta.

Ask the time

What's the time?
What time is it?

1. It's [It is] midnight. (24.00)
2. It's midday/twelve o'clock. (12.00)
3. It's one (o'clock)/one p.m. (13.00)

4. It's two (o'clock)/two a.m. (2.00)
5. It's three (o'clock)/three a.m. (3.00)
6. It's four (o'clock)/four a.m. (4.00)
7. It's five (o'clock)/five a.m. (5.00)
8. It's six (o'clock)/six a.m. (6.00)
9. It's seven (o'clock)/seven a.m. (7.00)
10. It's eight (o'clock)/eight a.m. (8.00)
11. It's nine (o'clock)/nine a.m. (9.00)
12. It's ten (o'clock)/ten a.m. (10.00)
13. It's eleven (o'clock)/eleven a.m. (11.00)
14. It's twelve (o'clock)/twelve a.m. (12.00)
15. It's one (o'clock)/one p.m. (13.00)
16. It's two (o'clock)/two p.m. (14.00)
17. It's three (o'clock)/three p.m. (15.00)
18. It's four (o'clock)/four p.m. 16.00)
19. It's five (o'clock)/five p.m. (17.00)

...

20. It's five (minutes) past two. (2.05)
21. It's ten (minutes) past two. (2.10)
22. It's a quarter past two/two fifteen. (2.15)
23. It's twenty (minutes) past two/two twenty. (2.20)
24. It's half past two/two thirty. (2.30)
25. It's twenty-five (minutes) to three. (2.35)

26. It's twenty (minutes) to three. (2.40)
27. It's a quarter to three/two forty-five. (2.45)

ሰዓት ምሕታት

ሰዓት ክንደይ ኮይኑ፧

1. ፍርቂ ለይቲ
2. ፍርቂ መዓልቲ
3. ሰዓት ሓደ

4. ሰዓት ክልተ ኮይኑ
5. ሰዓት ሰለስተ ኮይኑ
6. ሰዓት ኣርባዕተ ኮይኑ
7. ሰዓት ሓሙሽተ ኮይኑ
8. ሰዓት ሽዱሽተ ኮይኑ
9. ሰዓት ሸውዓተ ኮይኑ
10. ሰዓት ሸሞንተ ኮይኑ
11. ሰዓት ትሽዓት ኮይኑ
12. ሰዓት ዓሰርተ ኮይኑ
13. ሰዓት ዓሰርተ ሓደ ኮይኑ
14. ሰዓት ዓሰርተ ክልተ ኮይኑ
15. ሰዓት ሓደ ናይ ኣጋ ምሸት
16. ሰዓት ክልተ ናይ ኣጋ ምሸት
17. ሰዓት ሰለስተ ናይ ኣጋ ምሸት
18. ሰዓት ኣርባዕተ ናይ ኣጋ ምሸት
19. ሰዓት ሓሙሽተ ናይ ኣጋ ምሸት

...

20. ሰዓት ክልተን ሓሙሽተን
21. ሰዓት ክልተን ዓሰርተን
22. ሰዓት ክልተን ርብዕን
23. ሰዓት ክልተን ዕስራን
24. ሰዓት ክልተን ፈረቓን
25. ንሰዓት ሰለስተ ዕስራን ሓሙሽተን ጎደል
26. ንሰዓት ሰለስተ ዕስራ ጎደል
27. ንሰዓት ሰለስተ ርብዒ ጎደል

Chiedere l'ora

Che ora è?
Che ore sono?

1. E' mezzanotte.
2. E' mezzogiorno.
3. E' l'una.

4. Sono le due.
5. Sono le tre.
6. Sono le quattro.
7. Sono le cinque.
8. Sono le sei.
9. Sono le sette.
10. Sono le otto.
11. Sono le nove.
12. Sono le dieci.
13. Sono le undici.
14. Sono le dodici.
15. Sono le tredici.
16. Sono le quattordici.
17. Sono le quindici.
18. Sono le sedici.
19. Sono le diciassette.

...

20. Sono le due e cinque.
21. Sono le due e dieci.
22. Sono le due e quindici/un quarto.
23. Sono le due e venti.
24. Sono le due e trenta/mezzo.
25. Sono le due e trentacinque.

26. Sono le tre meno venti.
27. Sono le tre meno quindici/un quarto.

TRAVEL BY AIR OR SEA

HOW TO ...
1. Ask about times of departure and arrival
2. Buy tickets specifying: destination, single or return and class
3. Say where you would like to sit
4. Inform someone about your proposed times of arrival and departure

1.1 What time is the a flight for Venice?
1.2 What time does the boat leave for Genoa?
1.3 What time does the ferry leave for Messina?
1.4 What time does the ferry arrive in Messina?

2.1 I'd [I would] like a single ticket to Rome.
2.2 I'd like a return ticket.
2.3 In tourist class.
2.4 In first class.

ብኣየርን ባሕርን ጕዕዞ

ከመይ ጌርካ ...
1. ብዛዕባ ሰዓታት ንቕሎን ብጽሖን ከም እትሓትት
2. እትበጽሖ ቦታን: ዓይነትን ቲኬትን ፈሊኻ ከም እትገልጽ፧
3. ኣበይ ኮፍ ክትብል ከም እትደሊ ከም እትገልጽ
4. ንሓደ ሰብ ብዛዕባ ሰዓታት ጕዕዞ ከም እትሕብር

1.1 ሰዓት ክንደይ ኢዩ በረራ ንቬነስያ፧
1.2 ሰዓት ክንደይ ኢያ መርከብ ንጀኖቫ እትነቅል፧
1.3 መርከብ ሰዓት ክንደይ ኢያ ንመሲና እትነቅል፧
1.4 መርከብ ሰዓት ክንደይ ኢያ ኣብ መሲና እትበጽሕ፧

2.1 መኸዲ ቲኬት ንሮማ የድልየኒ ነይሩ
2.2 መኸድን መምለስን ቲኬት የድልየኒ ነይሩ
2.3 ኣብ ቱሪስት መዓርግ
2.4 ኣብ ቀዳማይ መዓርግ

VIAGGIARE IN AEREO O VIA NAVE

Come ...
1. chiedere gli orari di partenza e di arrivo
2. comprare biglietti specificando la destinazione, se di sola andata o di andata e ritorno e la classe
3. dire dove si desidera sedersi
4. informare qualcuno sull'orario di partenza e di arrivo

1.1 A che ora c'è un volo per Venezia?
1.2 A che ora parte la nave per Genova?
1.3 A che ora parte il traghetto per Messina?
1.4 A che ora arriva a Messina?

2.1 Vorrei un biglietto di andata per Roma.
2.2 Vorrei un biglietto di andata e ritorno.
2.3 In classe turistica.
2.4 In prima classe.

3.1 I'd like a seat next to the window.
3.2 I'd like a seat near the corridor.
3.3 I'd like a seat in a (non-)smoking compartment.

4.1 (At) what time are you leaving?
4.2 (At) what time is he/she leaving?
4.3 (At) what time are you leaving?
4.4 (At) what time are they leaving?
4.5 (At) what time are you arriving?

4.6 I'm leaving at six (o'clock).
4.7 He/she is leaving at seven.
4.8 We're [We are] leaving at eight.
4.9 They're leaving at nine.
4.10 I'm arriving at ten.

3.1 ኣብ ጥቓ መስኮት ኮፍ ክብል ምደለኹ
3.2 ኣብ ጥቓ ኮሪዶዮ ኮፍ ክብል ምደለኹ
3.3 ኣብ ሽጋራ ዝትከኽ / ዘይትከኽ ክፍሊ ኮፍ ክብል ምደለኹ

4.1 ሰዓት ክንደይ ኢኻ እትነቅል፧
4.2 ሰዓት ክንደይ ኢዩ ዚነቅል፧
4.3 ሰዓት ክንደይ ኢኹም እትነቕሉ፧
4.4 ሰዓት ክንደይ ኢዮም ዚነቕሉ፧
4.5 ሰዓት ክንደይ ኢኻ እትኣቱ፧

4.6 ሰዓት 6 ክነቅል እየ
4.7 ሰዓት 7 ኪነቅል ኢዩ
4.8 ሰዓት 8 ክንነቅል ኢና
4.9 ሰዓት 9 ኪነቅሉ/ላ ኢዮም/ኢየን
4.10 ሰዓት 10 ክኣቱ እየ

3.1 Vorrei un posto accanto al finestrino.
3.2 Vorrei un posto vicino al corridoio.
3.3 Vorrei un posto tra i (non) fumatori.

4.1 A che ora partirai?
4.2 A che ora partirà?
4.3 A che ora partirete ?
4.4 A che ora partiranno?
4.5 A che ora arriverai?

4.6 Partirò alle sei.
4.7 Partirà alle sette.
4.8 Partiremo alle otto.
4.9 Partiranno alle nove.
4.10 Arriverò alle dieci.

PRIVATE TRANSPORT

HOW TO ...
1. Buy petrol by grade, volume or price
2. Ask someone to check oil, water and tyres
3. Ask if there is a place nearby
4. Ask for technical help
5. Ask for a receipt

1.1 I'd like 20 pounds worth of (unleaded) petrol.
1.2 I'd like 60 pounds worth of diesel.
1.3 I'd like 20 litres of four star.
1.4 Fill it up, please.

2.1 Can you check the oil, please?
2.2 Can you check the water, please?
2.3 Can you check the tyres, please?
2.4 Can you check the tyre pressure, please?

ብሕታዊ መጎዓዝያ

ከመይ ጌርካ ...
1. በንዚና (ዓይነት ብዝሒ ዋጋ) ከም እትገዝእ
2. ዘይትን ማይን ጎማን ወዘተ ንኽሪኡልካ ከም እትሓትት
3. ሓደ ውሱን ቦታ ቀረባ ምዃኑ ከም እትሓትት
4. ተክኒካዊ ሓገዝ ከም እትሓትት
5. ቅብሊት ከም እትሓትት

1.1 ፒዮምቦ ዘይብሉ ዋጋ 240 ብር በንዚና ደልየ ነይረ
1.2 ዋጋ 200 ብር ናፍታ ደልየ ነይረ
1.3 20 ሊትሮ ፎርስታር ደልየ ነይረ
1.4 በንዚን ምመላእኩምለይዶ ብኽብረትኩም።
2.1 በጃኹም'ንዶ ዘይቲ ረኣዩለይ።
2.2 በጃኹም'ንዶ ማይ ረኣዩለይ።
2.3 በጃኹም'ንዶ ጎማ ረኣዩለይ።
2.4 በጃኹም'ንዶ ናይ ጎማ ጸቕጢ (ፕረስዮን) ረኣዩለይ።

TRASPORTO PRIVATO

Come ...
1. comprare la benzina (tipo, qualità e prezzo)
2. chiedere di controllare l'olio, l'acqua, le gomme, ecc.
3. chiedere se un determinato luogo è vicino
4. chiedere l'aiuto di un tecnico
5. chiedere la ricevuta

1.1 (Vorrei) 60.000 lire di benzina (senza piombo).
1.2 (Vorrei) 50.000 lire di diesel.
1.3 (Vorrei) 20 litri di super.
1.4 (Mi faccia) il pieno, per favore.
2.1 Mi controlli l'olio, per favore.
2.2 Mi controlli l'acqua, per favore.
2.3 Mi controlli le gomme, per favore.
2.4 Mi controlli la pressione delle gomme, per favore.

3.1 Is there a garage near here?
3.2 Is there a motorway near here?
3.3 Is there a car park near here?
3.4 Is there a car wash near here?

4.1 I need a mechanic.
4.2 My car has broken down.
4.3 I've [I have] got engine trouble.
4.4 My battery is flat.
4.5 I've run out of petrol.

5.1 Can you give me a receipt, please? 5.2 Here you are. Have a good journey!

3.1 ኣብዚ ቀረባ ጋራጅ ኣሎዶ፧
3.2 ኣብዚ ቀረባ ዓቢ ጽርግያ ኣሎዶ፧
3.3 ኣብዚ ቀረባ ናይ መኻይን ፓርክ ኣሎዶ፧
3.4 ኣብዚ ቀረባ መሕጸቢ መኪና ኣሎዶ፧

4.1 መካኒኮ የድልየኒ ኣሎ
4.2 መኪናይ ተሰቢራ
4.3 ሞቶረ ተበላሽዩኒ
4.4 ባተሪየይ ሞይቱ
4.5 በንዚና ወዲአ

5.1 ቅብሊት ክትሀቡኒ ምኽኣልኩምዶ፧ 5.2 እነሀ፡ ጽቡቕ መገሻ ይግበረልኩም

3.1 C'è un'officina qui vicino?
3.2 C'è un'autostrada qui vicino?
3.3 C'è un parcheggio qui vicino?
3.4 C'è un lavaggio qui vicino?

4.1 Ho bisogno di un meccanico.
4.2 Ho un guasto alla macchina.
4.3 Ho la macchina in panne.
4.4 Ho la batteria scarica.
4.5 Sono rimasta senza benzina.

5.1 Mi può dare la ricevuta, per favore? 5.2 Ecco a lei. Buon viaggio!

6 HOLIDAYS

HOW TO ...
1. Say and enquire about where you and others normally spend your holidays and how long they last
2. Say how you spend your holidays and with whom

1.1 Where do you usually go on holiday ?
1.2 Where do you usually spend your holidays?

1.3 Where are you going on holiday this year?
1.4 Where is he/she going on holiday this summer?
1.5 Where are you going on holiday this summer?
1.6 Where are they going on holiday this summer?

1.10 Usually I go to Italy.
1.11 Usually I go to the mountains.
1.12 Sometimes I go to the seaside.
1.13 Often I go abroad.

1.14 I'm going to Florence.
1.15 He/she is going to Florence.
1.16 We're going to Florence.
1.17 They're going to Florence.

1.18 I'm staying in England.

ዕረፍቲ / በዓላት

ከመይ ጌርካ ...
1. እዋን ዕረፍቲ ብሓፈሻ ኣበይን ክንደይ ጊዜ ከም ዘወስድን ከም እትገልጽን እትሓትትን
2. በዓላትካ ብኸመይን ምስ መንን ከም እተሕልፍ ከም እትገልጽ

1.1 መብዛሕትኡ ጊዜ ንዕረፍቲ ኣበይ ትኸይድ/ዲ፧
1.2 መብዛሕትኡ ጊዜ ዕረፍትኻ/ኺ ኣበይ ተሕልፎ/ፍዮ፧

1.3 ሎሚ ዓመት ንዕረፍቲ ናበይ ክትከይድ ኢኻ፧(m)
ሎሚ ዓመት ንዕረፍቲ ናበይ ክትከዲ ኢኺ፧ (f)
1.4 ሎሚ ክረምቲ ንዕረፍቲ ናበይ ክኸይድ ኢዩ፧(m)
ሎሚ ክረምቲ ንዕረፍቲ ናበይ ክትከይድ ኢያ፧ (f)
1.5 ሎሚ ክረምቲ ንዕረፍቲ ናበይ ክትከዱ ኢኹም፧(m)
ሎሚ ክረምቲ ንዕረፍቲ ናበይ ክትከዳ ኢኽን፧(f)
1.6 ሎሚ ክረምቲ ንዕረፍቲ ናበይ ክኸዱ ኢዮም፧(m)
ሎሚ ክረምቲ ንዕረፍቲ ናበይ ክኸዳ ኢየን ፧(f)

1.10 መብዛሕትኡ ግዜ ናብ ዓዲ ጣልያን እኸይድ
1.11 መብዛሕትኡ ጊዜ ኣብ ጎቦታት ኣሕልፎ
1.12 ሓድሓደ ግዜ ናብ ባሕሪ እወርድ
1.13 ዝበዝሐ ጊዜ ንወጻኢ እኸይድ

1.14 ንፊረንሰ ክኸይድ እየ(m) (f)

1.15 ንፊረንሰ ኪኸይድ ኢዩ (m)
ንፊረንሰ ክትከይድ ኢያ (f)
1.16 ንፊረንሰ ክንከይድ ኢና(m) (f)
1.17 ንፊረንሰ ኪኸዱ ኢዮም(m)
ንፊረንሰ ኪኸዳ ኢየን (f)
1.18 ኣብ ዓዲ እንግሊዝ ክተርፍ እየ

VACANZE

Come ...
1. dire e chiedere dove si trascorrono generalmente le vacanze e quanto tempo durano
2. dire come si trascorrono le vacanze e con chi

1.1 Dove vai di solito in vacanza?
1.2 Dove passi di solito le vacanze?

1.3 Dove andrai quest'anno in vacanza?
1.4 Dove andrà quest'estate in vacanza?
1.5 Dove andrete quest'estate in vacanza?
1.6 Dove andranno quest'estate in vacanza?

1.10 Di solito vado in Italia.
1.11 Di solito vado in montagna.
1.12 Qualche volta vado al mare.
1.13 Spesso vado all'estero.

1.14 Andrò a Firenze.
1.15 Andrà a Firenze.
1.16 Andremo a Firenze.
1.17 Andranno a Firenze.
1.18 Resterò in Inghilterra.

1.7 How long will you stay on holiday? 1.8 How long will you be on holiday?	1.19 Two weeks. 1.20 About a fortnight.
1.9 Where would you like to go on holiday?	1.21 I'd like to go to Italy. 1.22 I'd like to go to Adi Quala. 1.23 I'd like to go to Keren.
2.1 What do you usually do on holiday ? 2.2 What do you usually do during your holidays?	2.5 I go for walks. 2.6 I do some sport. 2.7 I go to the discotheque. 2.8 I go skiing. 2.9 I go to the seaside.
2.3 Who are you spending your holidays with? 2.4 Who are you going on holiday with?	2.10 (I'm going) with my friends. 2.11 (I'm going) with my parents.

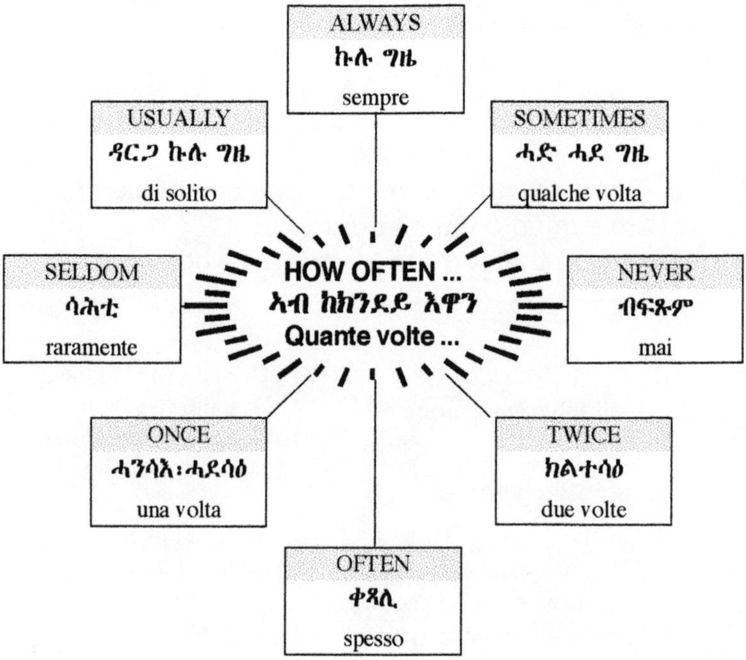

1.7 ንኽንደይ ግዜ ክትዕርፍ ኢኻ፧(m)
ንኽንደይ ግዜ ክትዕርፊ ኢኺ፧ (f)
1.8 ንኽንደይ ግዜ ኣብ ዕረፍቲ ክትጸንሕ ኢኻ/ ክትጸንሒ ኢኺ፧

1.19 ንኽልተ ሰሙን
1.20 ንኣስታት ክልተ ሰሙን

1.9 ንዕረፍቲ ናበይ ክትከይድ ምፈተኻ/ኺ፧

1.21 ንዓዲ ጣልያን ክኸይድ ምፈተኹ
1.22 ንዓዲ ዃላ ክኸይድ ምፈተኹ
1.23 ንከረን ክኸይድ ምፈተኹ

2.1 ኣብ እዋን ዕረፍቲ መብዛሕትኡ ግዜ እንታይ ትገብር/ሪ፧
2.2 ኣብ እዋን ዕረፍትኻ/ኺ መብዛሕትኡ ግዜ እንታይ ትገብር/ሪ፧

2.5 ብእግረይ እዛወር
2.6 ስፖርት እገብር
2.7 ናብ ዲስኮተክ እኸይድ
2.8 ኣብ በረድ እንሸራተት
2.9 ናብ ገምገም ባሕሪ እኸይድ

2.3 ዕረፍትኻ/ኺ ምስ መን ተሕልፎ/ፍዮ፧
2.4 ናብ ዕረፍትኻ/ኺ ምስ መን ክትከይድ/ዲ ኢኻ/ኢኺ፧

2.10 ምስ ኣዕሩኽይ እኸይድ
2.11 ምስ ስድራቤተይ እኸይድ

1.7 Per quanto tempo resterai in vacanza?
1.8 Per quanto tempo stai in vacanza?

1.19 Due settimane.
1.20 Una quindicina di giorni.

1.9 Dove ti piacerebbe andare in vacanza?

1.21 Mi piacerebbe andare in Italia.
1.22 Mi piacerebbe andare ad Adi Quala.
1.23 Mi piacerebbe andare a Cheren.

2.1 Che cosa fai di solito in vacanza?
2.2 Che cosa fai di solito durante le vacanze?

2.5 Faccio delle passeggiate.
2.6 Pratico qualche sport.
2.7 Vado in discoteca.
2.8 Vado a sciare.
2.9 Vado al mare.

2.3 Con chi passi le vacanze?
2.4 Con chi andrai in vacanza?

2.10 Con i miei amici.
2.11 Con i miei genitori.

7 TOURIST INFORMATION

HOW TO ...
1. Ask for information about a town and region
2. Ask for details of excursions
3. React (i.e. welcome or reject) to suggestions about activities

1.1 What places of interest are there to see ... ?
1.2 What are the city's main attractions?
1.3 There's a museum.
1.4 There's a sea-front promenade.
1.5 There are a lot of tourist itineraries.
1.6 There are a lot of historical monuments.

2.1 Do they organize any tourist itineraries?
2.2 Do they organize any excursions?
2.3 Could you recommend some excursions?
2.4 Could you recommend a guided tour?

ሓበሬታ ቱሪስት

ከመይ ጌርካ ...
1. ብዛዕባ ከተማን ከባቢኣን ከም እትሓትት
2. ናይ ጉዕዞ ዝርዝር ከም እትሓትት
3. ንንጥፈታትን ኣገደስቲ ቦታታትን ዝምልከቱ ሓሳባት ከም እትቕበሎን እትነጽጎን

1.1 እንታይ ኣገዳሲ ዚርአ ቦታታት ኣሎ፧
1.2 ናይዛ ከተማ ቀንዲ ሰሓብቲ ኣየኖት ኢዮም፧
1.3 ቤተመዘክር ኣሎ
1.4 ጐደና ገምገም ባሕሪ ኣሎ
1.5 ብዙሕ ናይ በጻሕቲ ሃገር መዛወሪታት ኣሎ
1.6 ብዙሕ ታሪኻዊ ቅርስታት ኣሎ

2.1 ዑደት በጻሕቲ ሃገር ይዳሎ ዲዩ፧
2.2 ዙረት ይዳሎ ዲዩ፧
2.3 ብዛዕባ ዙረት እንታይ ትመኽረኒ፧
2.4 ብዛዕባ ውጡን ዑደት እንታይ ትመኽረኒ፧

INFORMAZIONI TURISTICHE

Come ...
1. chiedere informazioni su una città o una regione
2. chiedere informazioni su escursioni
3. rispondere (es. accettare o rifiutare) a proposte di attività

1.1 Che cosa c'è di interessante da vedere in questa zona?
1.2 Quali sono le principali attrattive di questa città?
1.3 C'è il museo.
1.4 C'è la passeggiata a mare.
1.5 Ci sono molti itinerari turistici.
1.6 Ci sono molti monumenti storici.

2.1 Organizzano qualche giro turistico?
2.2 Organizzano delle escursioni?
2.3 Può consigliarmi delle escursioni?
2.4 Può consigliarmi delle visite guidate?

3.1 We could go to the museum.
3.2 We could go to the cinema.
3.3 You could go to the theatre.
3.4 Yes, that's a great idea.
3.5 No, I'm tired.
3.6 No, I don't feel like it.
3.7 No, I'm busy.

3.1 ናብ ቤተመዘክር ክንከይድ ንኽእል ኢና
3.2 ናብ ሲነማ ክንከይድ ንኽእል ኢና
3.3 ናብ ቴያትር ክትከይድ/ዲ ትኽእል/ሊ ኢኻ/ኺ
3.4 ጽቡቕ ሓሳብ
3.5 ኣይፋልን፡ ደኺመ ኣሎኹ
3.6 ደስ ኣይበለንን
3.7 ስራሕ ኣሎኒ

3.1 Potremmo andare al museo.
3.2 Potremmo andare al cinema.
3.3 Potresti andare a teatro.
3.4 Sì, è un'ottima idea.
3.5 No, sono stanco.
3.6 No, non ne ho voglia.
3.7 No, sono impegnato.

SOME SUGGESTIONS ABOUT THE DIFFERENT PARTS OF THE LETTER

INFORMAL	FORMAL
• Dear ...,	• To • Dear Mr./Mrs., • Dear Sir,
• Sorry I haven't written for ages ... • How are things? • You haven't written for ages ...	• I am/We are ... • The undersigned ... • This is to inform you ... • In answer to your letter of ... • With reference to your letter of ...
• I passed my exam ... • Why don't you come and see us ... • Could you do me a favour?	• I would be grateful if you could send us ... • We would be grateful if you could book ... • Please could you cancel ...
• Bye, bye. • Say hello to everyone from me. • Love and kisses, see you soon. • Lots of love (to everyone). • Love.	• Yours faithfully/sincerely. • Best regards/wishes. • I look forward to hearing from you. Yours faithfully.
• Name	• Name and surname
• Caro/a/i/e ...,	• A/Al/Alla/All' ..., • Caro/a Signor/a ..., • Egregio/Gentile Signore/a ...,
• Scusami se non ti ho scritto prima ... • Come va? • Da molto non mi scrivi ...	• Sono/Siamo ... • Il/La sottoscritto/a ... • Le/Vi comunico ... • In risposta alla Sua lettera del ... • Con riferimento alla Sua del ...
• Sono stato promosso ... • Perché non vieni a trovarci ... • Potresti farmi un favore?	• Le sarei grato se potesse inviarci ... • Vi saremmo grati se poteste prenotare ... • Vi preghiamo di annullare ...
• Ciao. • Saluta tutti da parte mia. Ciao. • Un bacio, a presto. • Tanti cari saluti (a tutti). • Affettuosi saluti.	• Distinti saluti. • Cordiali saluti. • In attesa di Vostre notizie, porgo distinti saluti.
• Nome	• Nome e cognome

8 HOTEL

HOW TO ...
1. Identify yourself
2. Say that you have (not) made a reservation
3. Ask if there are rooms available
4. State when you require a room and for how long
5. Ask the cost per night, per person, per room
6. Ask if meals are included
7. Say you would like to pay

1.1 Good morning. Can I help you?

1.2 Good morning, I'm Mr. Skelton.

2.1 I booked a room.
2.2 I have a room booked.
2.3 I haven't booked.

3.1 Do you have a single room?
3.2 Do you have a double room?

3.3 At the moment we're full.
3.4 For how long?
3.5 For how many nights?

4.1 From ... to ...
4.2 For one night.
4.3 For two weeks.

ሆቴል

ከመይ ጌርካ ...
1. ነብስኻ ከም እተፋልጥ
2. መደቀሲ ኣመዝጊብካ ከም እትጸንሕ
3. ናጻ ቦታ እንተድኣ ሃልዩ ከም እትሓትት
4. ንመዓስን ንኽንደይ እዋንን እታ መደቀሲት ከም እትደልያ ከም እትገልጽ
5. ዋጋ ሓንቲ መደቀሲት ንሓደ ሰብ ንሓንቲ ለይቲ ከም እትሓትት
6. መግቢ እቱው እንተ ኾይኑ ከም እትሓትት
7. ሕሳብ ንኽምጽኡልካ ከም እትሓትት

1.1 ከመይ ውዒልኩም፡ እንታይ ነይሩ፧

1.2 ከመይ ውዒልኩም ኣቶ ስከልቶን

2.1 ሓደ መደቀሲ ኣመዝጊበ ነይረ
2.2 ዝተመዝገበት ሓንቲ መደቀሲት ኣላትኒ
2.3 ኣየመዝገብኩን

3.1 ንሓደ ሰብ ዚኸውን ሓደ መደቀሲ ኣለኩምዶ፧
3.2 ናይ ክልተ ሰብ መደቀሲ ኣለኩምዶ፧

3.3 ንሕጂ ኩሉ ምሉእ ኢዩ
3.4 ንኽንደይ ጊዜ፧
3.5 ንኽንደይ ለይቲ፧

4.1 ካብ ... ክሳዕ
4.2 ንሓንቲ ለይቲ
4.3 ንኽልተ ቅነ

ALBERGHI

Come ...
1. presentarsi
2. dire se si è prenotato o no
3. chiedere se ci sono camere disponibili
4. dire per quando e per quanto tempo si richiede una camera
5. chiedere il costo per una notte, per persona, per camera
6. chiedere se i pasti sono inclusi
7. chiedere il conto

1.1 Buongiorno, desidera?

1.2 Buongiorno, sono il signor Skelton.

2.1 Ho prenotato una camera.
2.2 Ho una camera prenotata.
2.3 Non ho prenotato.

3.1 Avete una camera singola?
3.2 Avete una camera doppia?

3.3 Per il momento è tutto esaurito.
3.4 Per quanto tempo?
3.5 Per quante notti?

4.1 Dal ... al ...
4.2 Per una notte.
4.3 Per due settimane.

5.1 How much is it for one night ?
5.2 How much is it for one person?
5.3 How much is it for one room?
5.4 How much is it for full board?
5.5 How much is it for half board?

6.1 Is breakfast included?
6.2 Are meals included?
6.3 Yes, it's all included.
6.4 No, it's not included in the price.

7.1 (I would like) the bill, please.
7.2 Could you prepare the bill, please?
7.3 Here you are, thank you.

5.1 ክንደይ ኢዩ ዋግኡ ንሓንቲ ለይቲ፧
5.2 ክንደይ ኢዩ ዋግኡ ንሓደ ሰብ፧
5.3 ክንደይ ኢዩ ዋግኡ ንሓደ መደቀሲ፧
5.4 ክንደይ ኢዩ ዋግኡ ንምሉእ መስተንግዶ፧
5.5 ክንደይ ኢዩ ዋግኡ ንፍርቂ መስተንግዶ፧

6.1 ቁርሲ ኣብቲ ዋጋ እቱው ዲዩ፧
6.2 መግቢ ኣብቲ ዋጋ እቱው ዲዩ፧
6.3 እወ፡ ኩሉ እቱው ኢዩ
6.4 ኣይፋልን፡ እቱው ኣይኮነን

7.1 ብኽብረትኩም ሕሳብ ምደለኹ
7.2 ሕሳብዶ ምቐረብኩምለይ፧
7.3 እነሀለ፡ የቐንየለይ

5.1 Qual è il prezzo per una notte?
5.2 Qual è il prezzo per una persona?
5.3 Qual è il prezzo per una camera?

5.4 Quant'è la pensione completa?
5.5 Quant'è la mezza pensione?

6.1 E' compresa la prima colazione?
6.2 Sono compresi i pasti?
6.3 Sì, è tutto compreso.
6.4 No, non sono compresi nel prezzo.

7.1 (Vorrei) il conto, per favore.
7.2 Potrebbe prepararmi il conto, per favore?
7.3 Ecco a Lei, grazie.

Common words in hotels
ኣብ ሆቴላት እንጥቀመሉ ሓፈሻዊ ኣዘራርባ
Principali parole negli alberghi

drinking water	ዚስተ ማይ	acqua potabile
linen	ኣጫርቕ	biancheria
deposit	ተቐማጢ	caparra
safe	ካዝና	cassaforte
out of order	ካብ ጥቕሚ ወጻኢ	fuori servizio
half board	ፍርቂ መስተንግዶ	mezza pensione
youth hostel	ሆስተል መንእሰያት	ostello della gioventù
attended car-park	ሕሉው ፓርክ	parcheggio custodito
full board	ምሉእ መስተንግዶ	pensione completa
private beach	ሕዙእ ገምገም ባሕሪ	spiaggia privata
seaside resort	መዘናግዒ ገምገም ባሕሪ	stazione balneare
spa	ዘመናዊ ማይ ጸሎት	stazione termale
all included	ኩሉ ዝጠርነፈ	tutto compreso
emergency exit	ህጹጽ መውጽኢ	uscita di sicurezza
no camping	ተንዳ ኣይትትከሉ	vietato campeggiare
no admittance	ምእታው ክልኩል ኢዩ	vietato l'ingresso
no parking	ፓርኪን ክልኩል ኢዩ	vietato il parcheggio
board and lodging	ምግብን መደቀስን	vitto e alloggio
bed and breakfast	ዓራትን ቍርስን	alloggio e prima colazione

Reservations are valid only if they are made and confirmed in writing

ቦታ ኪተሓዝ ዚክኣል ኣቐዲምካ ብጽሑፍ ምስ እተመልክት ኢዩ

Le prenotazioni hanno valore solo se effettuate e confermate per iscritto

9 RESTAURANT

HOW TO ...
1. Ask for a table
2. Attract the waiter's attention
3. Order a drink or a snack
4. Order a meal
5. Express an opinion about a meal or dish
6. Ask for the bill

1.1 Hello, is that "Bologna" restaurant?

1.2 I'd [I would] like (to book) a table for two (people).
1.3 I'd like (to book) a table for five.

1. 4 For eight o'clock.

1.5 Yes, what can I do for you?

1.6 For what time?

1.7 Fine, what's your name?

ቤት መግቢ

ከመይ ጌርካ...
1. ጣውላ ከም እትሕዝ
2. ንኣሰላፊ ከም እትስሕቦ
3. መስተ ወይ ቍርሲ ከም እትእዝዝ
4. መግቢ ከም እትእዝዝ
5. ብዛዕባ ሓደ መግቢ ወይ ቢያቲ ሓሳባትካ ከም እትገልጽ
6. ሕሳብ ከም እትሓትት

1.1 ሃሎ፡ ቤት መግቢ ቦሎኛ ዲዩ፧

1.2 ንኽልተ ሰባት ቦታ ደልየ ነይረ

1.3 ንሓሙሽተ ሰባት ቦታ ደልየ ነይረ

1.4 ንሰዓት ሸሞንተ

1.5 እሺ፡ እንታይ ክእዘዝ፧

1.6 ንሰዓት ክንደይ፧

1.7 ግርም፡ መን ክብል፧

RISTORANTE

Come ...
1. **chiedere un tavolo**
2. **attirare l'attenzione del cameriere**
3. **ordinare una bevanda o uno spuntino**
4. **ordinare un pasto**
5. **esprimere un'opinione sul cibo**
6. **chiedere il conto**

1.1 Pronto, ristorante "Bologna"?

1.2 Vorrei (prenotare) un tavolo per due.
1.3 Vorrei (prenotare) un tavolo per cinque.

1.4 Per le otto.

1.5 Sì, dica!

1.6 Per che ora?

1.7 Va bene, qual è il Suo nome?

2.1 Waiter!
2.2 Waitress!

2.3 Yes, what would you like?

3.1 I'd like a coffee.
3.2 I'd like a cappuccino.
3.3 I'd like a sandwich.
3.4 I'd like a cheese roll.
3.5 I'd like a 'croissant'.
3.6 I'd like an orangeade.
3.7 I'd like a small pizza.
3.8 I'd like to see the menu.

4.1 (As a starter) I'd like ham and melon.
4.2 (As a starter) I'd like Russian salad.

2.1 ኣሰላፊ
2.2ኣሰላፊት

2.3 እሺ፡ እንታይ ክእዘዝ፡

3.1 ቡን ኣሎኩምዶ።
3.2 ካፑቺኖ ኣሎኩምዶ።
3.3 ፓኒኖ ኣሎኩምዶ።
3.4 ፎርማጆ ኣሎኩምዶ።
3.5 ብርዮሽ ኣሎኩምዶ።
3.6 ኣራንቻታ ኣሎኩምዶ።
3.7 ፒሳ ኣሎኩምዶ።
3.8 መኑ ክርእይ ምደለኹ

4.1 ከም ቅድመ መግቢ ፕሮሹቶን መሎንን ምደለኹ
4.2 ከም ቅድመ መግቢ ሰላጣ ሩስያ ምደለኹ

2.1 Cameriere!
2.2 Cameriera!

2.3 Prego! Desidera?

3.1 Vorrei un caffè.
3.2 Vorrei un cappuccino.
3.3 Vorrei un tramezzino.
3.4 Vorrei un panino al formaggio.
3.5 Vorrei un cornetto.
3.6 Vorrei un'aranciata.
3.7 Vorrei una pizzetta.
3.8 Vorrei vedere il menù.

4.1 Come antipasto vorrei del prosciutto e melone.
4.2 Come antipasto vorrei dell'insalata russa.

4.3 For first course I'd like (some) lasagna.
4.4 For first course I'd like (some) tagliatelle with tomato sauce.
4.5 For first course I'd like (some) spaghetti.

4.19 And what would you like to drink?

4.6 I'd like an orangeade.
4.7 I'd like a bottle of red/white wine.
4.8 I'd like some fizzy/natural mineral water.

4.9 (For the second course) what do you recommend?
4.10 (For the second course) what do you have?

4.20 I recommend the dish of the day.
4.21 I recommend this (dish).
4.22 I recommend the fried fish.

4.11 All right, I'll have this with mixed salad.
4.12 Thanks, but I prefer French fries.
4.13 Thanks, but I prefer cooked vegetables.

4.3 መጀመርታ ላዛኛ ምደለኹ
4.4 መጀመርታ ታልያተሊ ምስ ኮመደረ ምደለኹ

4.5 መጀመርታ ስፓገቲ ምደለኹ

4.19 እንታይከ ክትሰትዪ/ያ ትደልዪ/ያ፧

4.6 ኣራንቻታ ምደለኹ
4.7 ቀዪሕ/ጻዕዳ ቪኖ ምደለኹ
4.8 ጋዝ ዘለዎ/ዘይብሉ ማይ ምደለኹ

4.9 ከም ካልኣይ እንታይ ትመርጹለይ፧
4.10 ከም ካልኣይ እንታይ ኣሎኩም፧

4.20 ናይ ሎምመዓልቲ ፍሉይ መግቢ ይሕሸኩም
4.21 እዚ መግብዚ ይሕሸኩም
4.22 ቅሉው ዓሳ ይሕሸኩም

4.11 ሕራይ፡ ምስ ሕውስዋስ ሰላጣ ይኹን
4.12 የቐንየለይ፡ ግን ቅሉው ድንሽ ይሕሸኒ
4.13 የቐንየለይ፡ ግን እተቐልወ ኣሕምልቲ ይሕሸኒ

4.3 Come primo vorrei delle lasagne.
4.4 Come primo vorrei delle tagliatelle al pomodoro.
4.5 Come primo vorrei degli spaghetti.

4.19 E da bere (cosa desidera)?

4.6 Da bere vorrei un'aranciata.
4.7 Da bere vorrei una bottiglia di vino rosso/ bianco.
4.8 Da bere vorrei dell'acqua minerale (naturale/gassata).

4.9 Di secondo che cosa mi consiglia?
4.10 Di secondo che cosa avete?

4.20 Le consiglio il piatto del giorno.
4.21 Le consiglio questo piatto.
4.22 Le consiglio la frittura di pesce.

4.11 Va bene, prendo questo, con contorno di insalata mista.
4.12 Grazie, ma preferisco patatine fritte.
4.13 Grazie, ma preferisco verdure cotte.

4.14 Do you have any sweet/cake?
4.15 Do you have (any) ice-cream?
4.16 Do you have (any) cheese?
4.17 Do you have (any) fresh fruit?

4.23 I'm sorry, it's finished.

5.1 It's all very nice.
5.2 It's very nice.
5.4 The soup is too salty/needs more salt.
5.5 The meat is over-cooked/underdone.
5.6 The pizza is burnt.
5.7 The plate/glass is dirty.

6.1 Can I have the bill, please?

4.14 ፓስተ ኣለኩምዶ፧
4.15 ጀላቶ ኣለኩምዶ፧
4.16 ፎርማጆ ኣለኩምዶ፧
4.17 ሓድሽ ፍሩታ ኣለኩምዶ፧

4.23 ኣይትሓዙለይ፡ ተወዲኡ ኢዩ

5.1 ኩሉ ጥዑም ኢዩ
5.2 ኣዚዩ ጥዑም
5.4 እዚ መረቕ ጨው በዚሑዎ / እዚ መረቕ ጨው የድልዮ ኣሎ
5.5 እዛ ስጋ ብዙሕ ተቖልያ / እዛ ስጋ ብዙሕ ኣይተቐልወትን
5.6 እዛ ፒሳ ሓሪራ
5.7 እዚኣ ቢያቲ ረሳሕ ኢያ / እዚኣ ቢከሪ ረሳሕ ኢያ

6.1 ሕሳብዶ መምጻእካለይ፧

4.14 Avete del dolce?
4.15 Avete del gelato?
4.16 Avete del formaggio?
4.17 Avete della frutta fresca?

4.23 Ci dispiace, l'abbiamo finito.
4.24 Ci dispiace, l'abbiamo finita.

5.1 E' tutto molto buono.
5.2 E' buonissimo.
5.4 La minestra è salata/insipida.
5.5 La carne è troppo cotta/cruda.
5.6 La pizza è bruciata.
5.7 Il piatto/bicchiere è sporco.

6.1 Mi porta il conto, per favore?

Common words in recipes
ኣብ ምኽሻን ዚርከብ ቃላት
Principali parole nelle ricette

to toast, to roast	ምቕላው	abbrustolire
to slice, to cut	ምቕርዳድ	affettare
to add	ምውሳኽ	aggiungere
herbs	ቀመማት	aromi
to boil	ምጥጣቕ	bollire
saucepan	ባዴላ	casseruola
to cook	ምኽሻን	cuocere
to bake	ምስንካት	cuocere al forno
to stew	ምብሳል	cuocere in umido
to steam	ብሃፋ ምብሳል	cuocere a vapore
to grill	ምጥባስ	cuocere ai ferri
to fry	ምቕላው	friggere
to whisk, to whip	ምውቓዕ	frullare
to grate	ምፍሕፋሕ	grattugiare
to knead	ምልዋስ	impastare
to flour	ምጥሓን	infarinare
to rise	ምብኳዕ	lievitare
to mix, to stir	ምሕባር	mescolare
ladle	ምጮላፍ	mestolo
to put	ምእታው	mettere
breadcrumb	ርፍራፍ ባኒ	pane grattugiato
to peel	ምቕራፍ	pelare
stuffing	ምስጓድ	ripieno
to brown	ምቕያሕ	rosolare
to peel, to shell	ምቕራፍ/ምጮጫፍ	sbucciare
to fry lightly	ምጽላው	soffriggere
to squeeze	ምጽማቕ	spremere
to cut	ምምታር	tagliare
frying pan	ባዴላ	tegame
tureen, bowl	ጻሕሊ	terrina
to mince, to chop	ኣድቂቕካ ምምታር	tritare

10 SHOPPING

HOW TO ...

1. Find out about opening and closing times

2. Ask for information about supermarkets, shopping centres, etc.

3. Ask where specific departments are

4. Express quantity required (including expressions of weight, container; etc.)

5. Ask for particular items

6. Find out how much things cost

1.1 At what time do (clothes) shops open?

1.2 At what time do (clothes) shops close?

1.3 They open at eight thirty.

1.4 They close at...

2.1 Is there a supermarket?

2.2 Where's the shopping centre?

2.3 Where's the market?

ምግዛእን ምሽማትን

ከመይ ጌርካ ...
1. ብዛዕባ ምኽፋትን ምዕጻውን ድኳናት ሓበሬታ ከም እትሓትት
2. ብዛዕባ ሱፐርማርከት ሓበሬታ ከም እትሓትት
3. ፍሉይ ክፍሊ ኣበይ ከም ዚርከብ ከም እትሓትት
4. ብዛዕባ ብዝሕን ክብደትን ትሕዝቶን ከም እትገልጽ
5. ብዛዕባ ሓደ ፍሉይ ኣቕሓ ከም እትሓትት
6. ዋጋ ከም እትሓትት

1.1 ክዳውንቲ ዝሸየጠሉ ድኳን ሰዓት ክንደይ ይኽፈት፧
1.2 ክዳውንቲ ዝሸየጠሉ ድኳን ሰዓት ክንደይ ይዕጾ፧
1.3 ሰዓት ሸሞንተን ፈረቓን ይኽፍቱ
1.4 ሰዓት ... ይዓጽዉ

2.1 ኣብዚ ከባቢ፣ ሱፐርማርከት ኣሎዶ፧
2.2 ኣበይ ኢዩ ማእከል ዕዳጋ፧
2.3 ሹቕ ኣበይ ኢዩ፧

COMPERARE

Come ...
1. informarsi sugli orari di apertura e di chiusura
2. chiedere informazioni su supermercati, centri commerciali, ecc.
3. chiedere dove si trova un determinato reparto
4. esprimere la quantità richiesta
5. chiedere un particolare prodotto
6. chiedere il prezzo dei prodotti

1.1 A che ora aprono i negozi (di abbigliamento)?
1.2 A che ora chiudono i negozi (di abbigliamento)?
1.3 Aprono alle otto e mezzo.
1.4 Chiudono alle ...
2.1 C'è un supermercato?
2.2 Dov'è un centro commerciale?
2.3 Dov'è un mercato?

2.4 Where is a greengrocer's?
2.5 Where is a bureau de change/an exchange bureau?
2.6 Where is a chemist's?
2.7 Where is a butcher's?
2.8 Where is a baker's?
2.9 Where is a pastry shop?
2.10 Where is a jeweller's?

3.1 Where's the food department?
3.2 Where's the clothing department?
3.3 Where's the book department?
3.4 Where's the electrical department?

4.1 I'd like a litre of milk.
4.2 I'd like a kilo of bread.
4.3 I'd like a dozen eggs.
4.4 I'd like a plastic bag.
4.5 I'd like a bottle of wine.

2.4 መሸጣ ፍረታት ኣበይ ኢዩ ዚርከብ፧	2.4 Dov'è un fruttivendolo?
2.5 ገንዘብ ዝሸረፈሉ ቦታ ኣበይ ይርከብ፧	2.5 Dov'è una agenzia di cambio?
2.6 ፋርማሲ ኣበይ ይርከብ፧	2.6 Dov'è una farmacia?
2.7 እንዳ ስጋ ኣበይ ይርከብ፧	2.7 Dov'è una macelleria?
2.8 እንዳ ባኒ ኣበይ ይርከብ፧	2.8 Dov'è una panetteria?
2.9 እንዳ ፓስተ ኣበይ ኢዩ፧	2.9 Dov'è una pasticceria?
2.10 እንዳ ወርቂ በየን ኢዩ፧	2.10 Dov'è una gioielleria?
3.1 ናይ መግቢ ክፍሊ ኣበይ ይርከብ፧	3.1 Dov'è il reparto alimentari?
3.2 ናይ ክዳውንቲ ክፍሊ ኣበይ ይርከብ፧	3.2 Dov'è il reparto vestiti?
3.3 ናይ መጽሓፍቲ ክፍሊ ኣበይ ይርከብ፧	3.3 Dov'è il reparto libri?
3.4 ናይ ኤለክትሪክ ክፍሊ ኣበይ ይርከብ፧	3.4 Dov'è il reparto elettricità?
4.1 ሓደ ሊትሮ ጸባ ምደለኹ	4.1 Vorrei un litro di latte.
4.2 ሓደ ኪሎ ባኒ ምደለኹ	4.2 Vorrei un chilo di pane.
4.3 12 እንቋቝሖ ምደለኹ	4.3 Vorrei una dozzina di uova.
4.4 ሓንቲ ፌስታል ምደለኹ	4.4 Vorrei un sacchetto di plastica.
4.5 ጥርሙዝ ቪኖ ምደለኹ	4.5 Vorrei una bottiglia di vino.

5.1 I'd like a pullover.
5.2 I'd like a raincoat.
5.3 I'd like an umbrella.
5.4 I'd like a bag.
5.5 I'd like a jacket.
5.6 I'd like a coat.
5.7 I'd like a pair of shoes.

5.8 Made of nylon.
5.9 Made of leather.
5.10 Made of plastic.
5.11 Made of silk.
5.12 Made of cotton.

6.1 How much (is it)?

6.2 Can I pay by cheque?
6.3 Can I pay by credit card?

5.1 ጎልፎ ደልየ ነይረ
5.2 ናይ ዝናም ካፖት ደልየ ነይረ
5.3 ጽላል ደልየ ነይረ
5.4 ቦርሳ ደልየ ነይረ
5.5 ጃካ ደልየ ነይረ
5.6 ጁባ ደልየ ነይረ
5.7 ጫማ ደልየ ነይረ

5.8 ናይሎን
5.9 ብቈርበት እተሰርሐ
5.10 ብፕላስቲክ እተሰርሐ
5.11 ብሃሪ እተሰርሐ
5.12 ብጡጥ እተሰርሐ

6.1 እዚ ክንደይ'ዩ ዋግኡ፧

6.2 ብቸክ ክኽፍል እኽእልዶ፧
6.3 ብክረዲት ካርድ ክኽፍል እኽእልዶ፧

5.1 Vorrei un pullover.
5.2 Vorrei un impermeabile.
5.3 Vorrei un ombrello.
5.4 Vorrei una borsa.
5.5 Vorrei una giacca.
5.6 Vorrei un cappotto.
5.7 Vorrei un paio di scarpe.

5.8 Di nailon.
5.9 Di pelle.
5.10 Di plastica.
5.11 Di seta.
5.12 Di cotone.

6.1 Quanto costa?

6.2 Posso pagare con un assegno?
6.3 Posso pagare con la carta di credito?

11 SERVICES

POST OFFICE

HOW TO ...
1. Ask where a post office, a tobacconist or post box is.
2. Find out opening and closing times
3. Ask how much it costs to send letters, postcards or parcels to a particular country
4. Buy stamps of a particular value
5. Say whether you would like to send letters, postcards or parcels

1.1 Excuse me, where is a post office?
1.2 Excuse me, where is a tobacconist's?
1.3 Excuse me, where is a post box?

1.4 It's there, near the bank.
1.5 It's down there, on the right.
1.6 I'm sorry, I don't know.

2.1 At what time does the post office open?
2.2 At what time does the post office close?

2.3 It opens at eight fifteen.
2.4 It closes at 2.00 pm.

ቤት ፖስታ

ከመይ ጌርካ...

1. ቤት ፖስታ፡ እንዳ ሽጋራ ወይ ሳጹን ፓስታ ኣበይ ከም ዚርከብ ከም እትሓትት
2. ዚኸፈተሉን ዚዕጸወሉን ግዜ ከም እትሓትት
3. ደብዳበታት ካርቶሊናታት ባኮታት ናብ እተወሰነ ሃገር ንምስዳድ ክንደይ ከም ዚወስድ ከም እትሓትት
4. ውሱን ዋጋ ዘለዎም ቴምብራት ከም እትገዝእ
5. ብደብዳበ ብካርቶሊና ወይ ብካርድ ክትጽሕፍ ከም እትደሊ ከም እትገልጽ

1.1 ይቕረታ፡ ቤት ፖስታ ኣበይ ኢዩ፧
1.2 ይቕረታ፡ እንዳ ሽጋራ ኣበይ ኢዩ፧
1.3 ይቕረታ፡ ፖስታ ዚኣትዎ ሳጹን ኣበይ ኢዩ፧
1.4 ኣብቲ፡ ጥቓ ባንክ
1.5 ንታሕቲ፡ ንየማን ገጽካ
1.6 ኣይትሓዘለይ፡ ኣይፈልጦን እየ

2.1 ቤት ፖስታ ሰዓት ክንደይ ይኸፈት፧
2.2 ቤት ፖስታ ሰዓት ክንደይ ይዕጾ፧
2.3 ሰዓት ሸሞንተን ርብዕን ይኸፈት
2.4 ሰዓት ክልተ ናይ ኣጋ ምሸት ይዕጾ

UFFICIO POSTALE

Come ...

1. **chiedere dov'è un ufficio postale, una tabaccheria o una buca della lettere**
2. **informarsi sugli orari di apertura e di chiusura**
3. **chiedere quanto costa spedire una lettera, una cartolina o un pacco in un determinato paese**
4. **comprare francobolli di un determinato valore**
5. **dire se si desidera spedire lettere, cartoline o pacchi**

1.1 Scusi, dov'è un ufficio postale?
1.2 Scusi, dov'è una tabaccheria?
1.3 Scusi, dov'è una buca delle lettere?
1.4 E' là, vicino alla banca.
1.5 E' laggiù, sulla destra.
1.6 Non lo so, mi dispiace.

2.1 A che ora apre l'ufficio postale?
2.2 A che ora chiude l'ufficio postale?
2.3 Apre alle otto e quindici.
2.4 Chiude alle quattordici.

3.1 How much is it to send a letter to Germany?
3.2 How much is it to send a card to Belgium?
3.3 How much is it to send a parcel to Ireland?
3.4 How much is it to send a greeting card?

4.1 Would you give me a stamp for Great Britain, please?
4.2 Would you give me a stamp for a letter, please?
4.3 Would you give me a stamp for a card, please?

5.1 I'd like to send this letter by air-mail to Holland.
5.2 I'd like to send this parcel to Denmark.
5.3 I'd like to send a registered letter (with advice of receipt) to Australia.

3.1 ዋጋ መልኣኺ ደብዳበ ንጀርመን ክንደይ ይበጽሕ፧
3.2 ዋጋ መልኣኺ ካርድ ንበልጁም ክንደይ ይበጽሕ፧
3.3 ዋጋ መልኣኺ ፓርሰል ንኣየርላንድ ክንደይ ይበጽሕ፧
3.4 ዋጋ መልኣኺ ናይ ሰላምታ ካርድ ክንደይ ይበጽሕ፧

4.1 በጃኻ፡ ቴምብር ንብሪጣንያ ምሃብካኒዶ፧
4.2 በጃኻ፡ ቴምብር ንደብዳበ ምሃብካኒዶ፧
4.3 በጃኻ፡ ቴምብር ንካርድ ምሃብካኒዶ፧

5.1 ነዛ ደብዳበ ንሆላንድ ብኣየር ክልእካ ደልየ ነይረ
5.2 ነዛ ካርድ ንደንማርክ ክልእካ ደልየ ነይረ
5.3 ናይ ሓደራ ደብዳበ ንኣውስትራልያ ክልእኽ ደልየ ነይረ

3.1 Quanto costa spedire una lettera in Germania?
3.2 Quanto costa spedire una cartolina in Belgio?
3.3 Quanto costa spedire un pacco in Irlanda?
3.4 Quanto costa spedire un biglietto d'auguri?

4.1 Mi dia un francobollo per la Gran Bretagna, per favore.
4.2 Mi dia un francobollo per lettera, per favore.
4.3 Mi dia un francobollo per cartolina, per favore.

5.1 Vorrei spedire questa lettera per via aerea in Olanda.
5.2 Vorrei spedire questo pacco in Danimarca.
5.3 Vorrei spedire una raccomandata (con ricevuta di ritorno) in Australia.

TELEPHONE

HOW TO ...
1. Give and seek information about where phone calls can be made
2. Ask if you can make a call
3. Ask for a telephone number
4. Answer a phone call
5. Make a phone call and ask to speak to someone

1.1 Where's the nearest phone-box?
1.2 Where's the nearest public phone?

1.2 In Piazza Dante, next to the newspaper kiosk.
1.3 A hundred metres on your right.

2.1 Can I make a phone call to my parents?
2.2 Could I make a phone call?
2.3 Can I phone Sandra?

2.4 Yes, of course!

3.1 What's your phone number?
3.2 What is the code for Florence?
3.3 What number do I have to dial for Great Britain?

3.4 My number is (0184) 357136.
3.5 The code for Florence is 055.

4.1 Hello!
4.2 Hello! Who's speaking?

4.3 This is Mr. Haile.
4.4 This is Anna.

5.1 Could I speak to Dr. Brandi?
5.2 Is Sonia there?

5.3 I can't hear you, please speak louder!
5.4 Yes, one moment!
5.5 Yes, it's me.
5.6 I'll [I will] call him for you.
5.7 I'll call her for you.
5.8 You've got the wrong number.
5.9 I'm sorry, but he has just gone out.
5.10 Could you phone tonight?
5.11 Could you call back later?
5.12 Could you call back in ten minutes?

ተለፎን

ከመይ ጌርካ ...
1. ኣበይ ከም ዚድወል ሓበሬታ ከም እትህብን እትውክስን
2. ንምድዋል ፍቓድ እንተሎ ከም እትሓትት
3. ቍጽሪ ተለፎን ከም እትሓትት
4. መልሲ ተለፎን ከም እትቕበል
5. ደዊልካ ምስ ካልእ ሰብ ንኽትዛረብ ከም እትሓትት

1.1 ሳንዱቕ ተለፎን ኣበየናይ ከባቢ ይርከብ፧
1.2 ህዝባዊ ተለፎን ኣበየናይ ከባቢ ይርከብ፧
1.2 ኣብ ፒያሳ ዳንተ፡ ድሕሪ መሸጣ ጋዜጣ
1.3 ሚእቲ መትሮ ንየማንካ

2.1 ናብ ስድራይ ተለፎን ክድውል እኽእል ድየ፧
2.2 ናብ ሳንድራ ተለፎን ክድውልዶ፧
2.3 ክድውል እኽእልዶ፧
2.4 እወ፡ ከመይ ደኣ

3.1 ቍጽሪ ተለፎንካ ክንደይ ኢዩ፧
3.2 ኮድ ናይ ፍሎረንስ ክንደይ ኢዩ፧
3.3 ኣየናይ ቍጽሪ ክወስድ ናብ ዓባይ ብሪጣንያ ንምድዋል፧
3.4 ቍጽሪ ተለፎነይ (0184) 357136 ኢዩ
3.5 ኮድ ናይ ፍሎረንስ 055 ኢዩ

4.1 ሃለው
4.2 ሃለው፡ መን ኢዩ ዚዛረብ ዘሎ
4.3 ሚስተር ሃይለ እየ
4.4 ኣና እየ

5.1 ምስ ዶክተር ብራንዲ ክዛረብ ምኽእልኩዶ፧
5.2 ሶኒያ ኣብኡ ኣላዶ፧
5.3 ኣይሰምዓካን እየ ዘለኹ፡ ዓው ኢልካ ተዛረብ
5.4 እወ፡ ሓንሳብ
5.5 እወ፡ ኣነ እየ
5.6 ክጽወዓልካ እየ
5.7 ክጽወዓልካ እየ
5.8 ቍጽሪ ተጋጊኻ
5.9 ኣይትሓዘለይ፡ ሕጂ ሕጂ ወጺኡ/ወጺኣ
5.10 ሎም ምሸት ክትድውል ምኽኣልካዶ፧
5.11 ጸኒሕካ ክትድውል ምኽኣልካዶ፧
5.12 ድሕሪ ዓሰርተ ደቓቕ ክትድውል ምኽኣልካዶ፧

TELEFONO

Come ...
1. dare e chiedere informazioni su dove si può telefonare
2. chiedere se si può telefonare
3. chiedere un numero di telefono
4. rispondere ad una telefonata
5. telefonare e chiedere di parlare con qualcuno

1.1 Dov'è una cabina telefonica?
1.2 Dov'è un telefono (pubblico)?

1.2 In Piazza Dante, accanto all'edicola.
1.3 A cento metri, sulla destra.

2.1 Posso fare una telefonata ai miei genitori?
2.2 Posso telefonare a Sandra?
2.3 Potrei telefonare?

2.4 Sì, certamente!

3.1 Qual è il Suo numero di telefono?
3.2 Qual è il prefisso di Firenze?
3.3 Che numero devo fare per la Gran Bretagna?

3.4 Il mio numero di telefono è (0184) 357136.
3.5 Il prefisso di Firenze è 055.

4.1 Pronto!
4.2 Pronto! Chi parla?

4.3 Sono il signor Haile.
4.4 Sono Anna.

5.1 Potrei parlare con il dottor Brandi?
5.2 C'è Sonia?

5.3 Non la sento, parli più forte!
5.4 Sì, un attimo!
5.5 Dica! Sono io.
5.6 Glielo chiamo.
5.7 Gliela chiamo.
5.8 Ha sbagliato numero.
5.9 Mi dispiace, ma è appena uscito.
5.10 Potrebbe telefonare stasera?
5.11 Potrebbe richiamare più tardi?
5.12 Potrebbe richiamare tra dieci minuti?

BANK

HOW TO ...
1. Say you would like to change travellers' cheques or money
2. Ask for coins or notes of a particular denomination

1.1 I'd like to change some travellers' cheques.
1.2 I'd like to change dollars.
1.3 I'd like to change lire.
1.4 I'd like to change pounds.

1.9 Have you any means of identification?

1.5 Yes, I have my passport.

1.10 Sign here, please!

1.6 What is the exchange rate for the Australian Dollar?
1.7 What is the exchange rate for the Pound?
1.8 What is the exchange rate for the Yen?

2.1 Could you give me some ten thousand lire notes?
2.2 Could you give me two five thousand lire notes?
2.3 Could you give me some change?

2.7 And the change, how would you like it?

2.4 I would like it in thousand lire notes.
2.5 It doesn't matter!
2.6 As you like!

ባንካ

ከመይ ጌርካ ...
1. ናይ ጉዕዞ ቸክ ወይ ገንዘብ ከተሸርፎ ትደሊ ምኻንካ ከም እትገልጽ
2. ውሱን ዋጋ ዘለዎ ዝርዝርን ጥቕሉልን ገንዘብ ከም እትሓትት

1.1 ካብዚ ናይ ጉዕዞ ቸክ ቅሩብ ክቕይር ደልየ ነይረ
1.2 ዶላር ክቐይር ደልየ ነይረ
1.3 ሊረ ክቐይር ደልየ ነይረ
1.4 ፓውንድ ክቐይር ደልየ ነይረ

1.5 እወ፡ ፓስፖርት ኣሎኒ

1.6 ገንዘብ ኣውስትራልያ ክንደይ ይሸረፍ፧
1.7 ሓደ ፓውንድ ክንደይ ይሸረፍ፧
1.8 ሓደ የን ክንደይ ይሸረፍ፧

1.9 ሰነዳት ኣሎካዶ፧

1.10 ብኽብረትካ ኣብዚ ፈርም

2.1 ናይ ዓሰርተ ሽሕ ሊረ ጥቕሉል ምሃብካኒዶ፧
2.2 ነናይ ክልተ ሽሕ ሊረ ጥቕሉል ምሃብካኒዶ፧
2.3 ቁሩብ ዝርዝር ምሃብካኒዶ፧

2.4 ነናይ ሓደ ሽሕ ሊረ ጥቕሉል ደልየ ኣለኹ
2.5 ጸገም የለን
2.6 ከም ድላይካ

2.7 እቲ ዝተረፈ ብኸመይ ኢኻ እትደልዮ፧

BANCA

Come ...
1. dire se si desidera cambiare travellers' chèque o valuta
2. chiedere monete o banconote di un determinato valore

1.1 Vorrei cambiare dei travellers' chèque.
1.2 Vorrei cambiare dei dollari.
1.3 Vorrei cambiare delle lire.
1.4 Vorrei cambiare delle sterline.

1.9 Ha un documento, per favore?

1.5 Sì, ho il passaporto.

1.10 Firmi qui, per favore.

1.6 Quant'è il cambio del dollaro australiano?
1.7 Quant'è il cambio della sterlina?
1.8 Quant'è il cambio dello yen?

2.1 Potrebbe darmi dei biglietti da diecimila?
2.2 Potrebbe darmi due biglietti da cinquemila?
2.3 Potrebbe darmi della moneta?

2.7 E il resto come lo vuole?

2.4 Vorrei dei biglietti da mille (lire).
2.5 Non importa!
2.6 Come vuole lei!

SIGNS AND KEY WORDS

CHEQUE	Assegno
TRAVELLER'S CHEQUE	Assegno turistico
	Travellers' cheque
BANK	Banca
BILL, NOTE	Bolletta
STOCK EXCHANGE	Borsa
EXCHANGE	Cambio
CHEQUE CARD	Carta assegni
CREDIT CARD	Carta di credito
CASH DESK	Cassa
NIGHT SAFE	Cassacontinua
SAVING BANK	Cassa di risparmio
SAFE DEPOSIT BOX	Cassetta di sicurezza
TO ENDORSE	Girare
CHEQUE BOOK	Libretto di assegni
FORM	Modulo
COIN	Moneta
LOAN	Mutuo
TO CASH	Riscuotere
TO PAY	Versare
SMALL CHANGE	Spiccioli
COUNTER	Sportello
CASH TILL	Sportello automatico
FOREIGN CURRENCY	Valute estere

12 HEALTH

HOW TO ...
1. State how you feel
2. Refer to parts of the body where you are in pain or discomfort
3. Report minor ailments
4. Report injuries
5. Ask for items in a chemist's
6. Call for help
7. Warn about danger

1.1 How are you?
1.2 How is it going?
1.3 How do you feel?

1.4 I am well/I'm fine.
1.5 I am not well/I don't feel well.
1.6 I feel weak.
1.7 I feel better.

2.1 What's wrong with you?
2.2 What's wrong?

2.3 I've got toothache.
2.4 I've got a sore throat.

ጥዕና

ከመይ ጌርካ ...

1. ከመይ ከም ዚስመዓካ ከም እትገልጽ
2. ቃንዛ ወይ ጽልኣት ኣበይ ከም ዚስመዓካ ከም እትሕብር
3. ብዛዕባ ነኣሽቱ ሕማማት ከም እትገልጽ
4. ማህሰይትኻ ከም እትገልጽ
5. ኣብ ቤት መድሃኒት፡ መድሃኒት ከም እትሓትት
6. ረዲኤት ከም እትሓትት
7. ብዛዕባ ሓደጋ መጠንቀቕታ ከም እትህብ

1.1 ከመይ ኣሎኻ/ኺ፧
1.2 ከመይ ኣሎ ኩነታት፧
1.3 ከመይ ይስመዓካ/ኪ፧

1.4 ጽቡቕ ኣሎኹ
1.5 ሕማቕ ኣሎኹ
1.6 ኣዚዩ ድኻም ይስመዓኒ
1.7 ይሕሸኒ ኣሎ

2.1 እንታይ ኰንካ/ኪ፧
2.2 ገለ ኰንካ ኣሎኻ ገለ/ ኰንኪ ኣሎኺ፧

2.3 ሕማም ስኒ ኣሎኒ
2.4 ጎረሮይ የሕምመኒ ኣሎ

SALUTE

Come ...

1. dire come ci si sente
2. dire dove si prova dolore o fastidio
3. riferire ad altri su piccoli malesseri
4. dire ad altri che ci si è fatti male
5. chiedere un determinato prodotto in farmacia
6. chiedere aiuto
7. avvertire di un pericolo

1.1 Come stai?
1.2 Come va?
1.3 Come ti senti?

1.4 (Sto) bene.
1.5 (Sto) male.
1.6 Mi sento debole.
1.7 Mi sento meglio.

2.1 Che cos'hai?
2.2 Cos'è che non va?

2.3 Ho mal di denti.
2.4 Ho mal di gola.

2.5 I've got stomach-ache.
2.6 I've got backache.
2.7 I've got a headache.
2.8 My feet hurt.
2.9 My eyes hurt.

2.10 I'm hot.
2.11 I'm cold.
2.12 I'm hungry.
2.13 I'm thirsty.

3.1 Where does it hurt?
3.2 What symptoms do you have?

3.3 I have a pain here.
3.4 I've got cramps.
3.5 I've got sun-stroke.
3.6 I've got diarrhoea.
3.7 I've vomited.
3.8 I have a temperature.
3.9 I've got flu.
3.10 I've got high/low blood pressure.

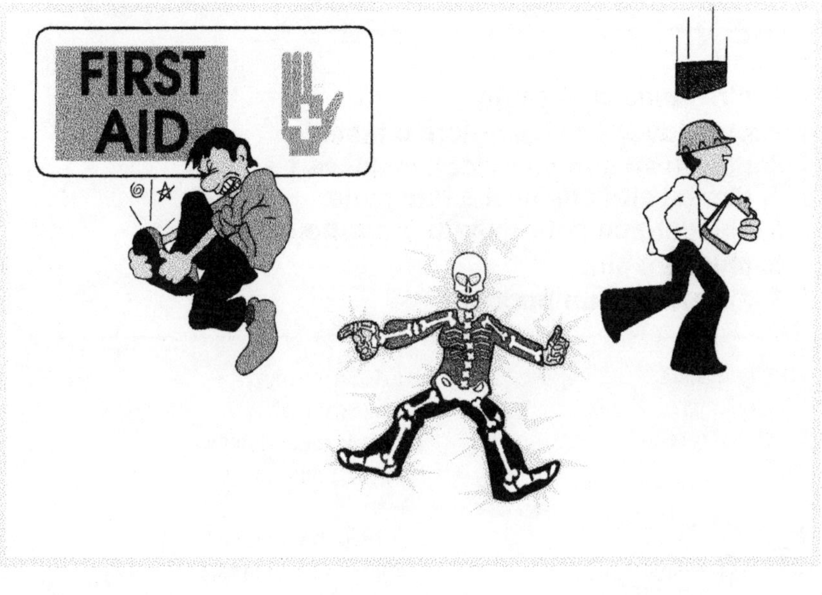

2.5 ከብደይ የሕምመኒ ኣሎ
2.6 ሕቘይ የሕምመኒ ኣሎ
2.7 ርእሰይ የሕምመኒ ኣሎ
2.8 ኣእጋረይ የሕምመኒ ኣሎ
2.9 ዓይነይ የሕምመኒ ኣሎ

2.10 ሃሩር ይስመዓኒ ኣሎ
2.11 ቁሪ ይስመዓኒ ኣሎ
2.12 ጠምየ ኣሎኹ
2.13 ጸሚአ ኣሎኹ

3.1 ኣበይ የሕምመካ ኣሎ/ ኣበይ የሕምመኪ ኣሎ፧
3.2 እንታይ ይስመዓካ ኣሎ /እንታይ ይስመዓኪ ኣሎ፧

3.3 ኣብዚ ቃንዛ ኣሎኒ
3.4 ቅርጥማት ኣሎኒ
3.5 ጸሓይ ሃሪማትኒ
3.6 ውጽኣት ኣሎኒ
3.7 ኣምሊሱኒ
3.8 ረስኒ ኣሎኒ
3.9 ጉንፋዕ ኣላትኒ
3.10 ጸቕጢ ደም/ዋሕዲ ደም ኣሎኒ

2.5 Ho mal di pancia.
2.6 Ho mal di schiena.
2.7 Ho mal di testa.
2.8 Ho male ai piedi.
2.9 Ho male agli occhi.

2.10 Ho caldo.
2.11 Ho freddo.
2.12 Ho fame.
2.13 Ho sete.

3.1 Dove ha male?
3.2 Che disturbi ha?

3.3 Ho un dolore qui.
3.4 Ho i crampi.
3.5 Ho preso un colpo di sole.
3.6 Ho la diarrea.
3.7 Ho rimesso.
3.8 Ho la febbre.
3.9 Ho l'influenza.
3.10 Ho la pressione alta/bassa.

4.1 I've burnt myself.
4.2 I've hurt myself.
4.3 I've injured myself.
4.4 I've pricked myself.
4.5 I've cut myself.

5.1 I would like some aspirin.
5.2 I would like some bandages.
5.3 I would like some plasters.
5.4 I would like some tablets.
5.5 I would like cotton-wool.
5.6 I would like a cough syrup.
5.7 I would like something for a head-ache.
5.8 I would like something to treat a burn/scald.
5.9 I would like something for an insect bite.

5.10 Take one spoonful of this medicine twice a day.
5.11 Take three drops ... every two hours.
5.12 Take one tablet before each meal.
5.13 Take half a dose ... in the evening.

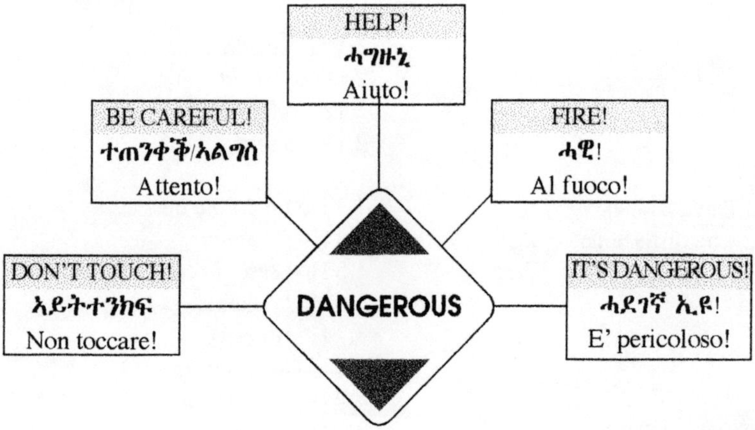

4.1 ሓዊ ነዲደ
4.2 ተሃስየ
4.3 ተጐዲአ
4.4 ተወጊአ
4.5 ተሓሪደ

5.1 ኣስፒሪን ኣሎኩምዶ፧
5.2 ባንደጅ ኣሎኩምዶ፧
5.3 ፕላስተር ኣሎኩምዶ፧
5.4 ኪኒና ኣሎኩምዶ፧
5.5 ጡጥ ኣሎኩምዶ፧
5.6 ናይ ሰዓል ሽሮፖ ኣሎኩምዶ፧
5.7 ዝኾነ ንሕማም ርእሲ ዚኸውን ፈውሲ ኣሎኩምዶ፧
5.8 ዝኾነ ንመንደድቲ ዚኸውን ፈውሲ ኣሎኩምዶ፧
5.9 ንመንከስቲ ሓሳኹ ዚኸውን ፈውሲ ኣሎኩምዶ፧

5.10 ካብዚኣ መድሃኒት ሓንቲ ማንካ 2 ግዜ ንመዓልቲ ውሰዱ
5.11 3 ነጥቢ ኣብ ክክልተ ሰዓት ውሰዱ
5.12 ሓንቲ ኪኒና ቅድሚ ነፍስ ወከፍ ምግቢ ውሰዱ
5.13 ምሸት ፍርቂ ዶዝ ... ውሰዱ

4.1 Mi sono bruciato.
4.2 Mi sono fatto male.
4.3 Mi sono ferito.
4.4 Mi sono punto.
4.5 Mi sono tagliato.

5.1 Vorrei delle aspirine.
5.2 Vorrei delle bende.
5.3 Vorrei dei cerotti.
5.4 Vorrei delle compresse.
5.5 Vorrei del cotone.
5.6 Vorrei dello sciroppo per la tosse.
5.7 Vorrei qualcosa per il mal di testa.
5.8 Vorrei qualcosa per le scottature.
5.9 Vorrei qualcosa per le punture d'insetti.

5.10 Prenda un cucchiaino di questa medicina due volte al giorno.
5.11 Prenda tre gocce ... ogni due ore.
5.12 Prenda una compressa prima dei pasti.
5.13 Prenda metà dose ... la sera.

13 FREE TIME

HOW TO ...
1. Say what your hobbies and interests are and inquire about those of others
2. Discuss your evening, weekend and holiday activities
3. Express simple opinions about TV, films, etc.
4. Find out the starting and finishing time (of a film or concert)

1.1 What is your favourite hobby?
1.2 How do you spend your free time?
1.3 What do you do in your free time?

1.5 (I like) collecting stamps.
1.6 (I like) collecting post cards.
1.7 (I like) playing draughts.
1.8 (I like) playing chess.
1.9 (I like) playing cards.
1.10 (I like) playing billiards.

Billiards
I like playing chess.

ናጻ ግዜ

ከመይ ጌርካ...
1. ድሌትካን መሕለፍ ግዜኻን እንታይ ምዃኑ ከም እትጋልጽ ናይ ካልኦት'ውን ከም እትሓትት
2. ምሸትን ቀዳመ ሰንበትን ግዜ ዕረፍትን ከመይ ከም እተሕልፎ ከም እትገልጽ
3. ብዛዕባ ተለቪዥን፡ ፊልም ወዘተ ዘሎካ ርእይቶ ከም እትገልጽ
4. ብዛዕባ ፊልም ወይ ኮንሰርት ዚጅመረሉን ዚውደኣሉን ሰዓታት ከም እትሓትት

1.1 እቲ ዝስሕበካ መሕለፍ ግዜ ኣየናይ ኢዩ፧
1.2 ትርፊ ግዜኻ ከመይ ጌርካ ተሕልፎ፧
1.3 ኣብ ትርፊ ግዜኻ እንታይ ትገብር፧
1.5 ቴምብር ፖስታ ምእካብ ደስ ይብለኒ
1.6 ካርቶሊናታት ምእካብ ደስ ይብለኒ
1.7 ዳማ ምጽዋት ደስ ይብለኒ
1.8 ቸስ ምጽዋት ደስ ይብለኒ
1.9 ካርታ ምጽዋት ደስ ይብለኒ
1.10 ቢልያርዶ ምጽዋት ደስ ይብለኒ

TEMPO LIBERO

Come ...
1. dire quali sono i propri passatempi e interessi e chiederlo ad altri
2. discutere di quello che si fa la sera, il fine settimana e durante le vacanze
3. esprimere opinioni sulla TV, sui film, ecc.
4. informarsi sull'orario di inizio e di fine di un film o di un concerto

1.1 Qual è il tuo passatempo preferito?
1.2 Come passi il tuo tempo libero?
1.3 Che cosa fai nel tempo libero?
1.5 Mi piace collezionare francobolli.
1.6 Mi piace collezionare cartoline.
1.7 Mi piace giocare a dama.
1.8 Mi piace giocare a scacchi.
1.9 Mi piace giocare a carte.
1.10 Mi piace giocare a biliardo.

	1.11 (I like) photography. 1.12 (I like) model making. 1.13 (I like) computers. 1.14 (I like) football. 1.15 (I like) music. 1.16 (I like) playing the guitar. 1.17 (I like) ballet. 1.18 (I like) walking.
1.4 Do you do any sport?	1.19 Yes, I go cross-country running. 1.20 Yes, I do high-jumps. 1.21 Yes, I go swimming. 1.22 Yes, I go cycling. 1.23 Yes, I play football. 1.24 Yes, I play tennis. 1.25 Yes, I play basketball. 1.26 Yes, I play handball. 1.27 Yes, I play rugby.

What's your favourite sport?

1.11 ፎቶግራፍ ደስ ይብለኒ
1.12 ስነ ጥበብ ደስ ይብለኒ
1.13 ኮምፕዩተር ደስ ይብለኒ
1.14 ኵዕሶ እግሪ ደስ ይብለኒ
1.15 ሙዚቃ ደስ ይብለኒ
1.16 ጊታር ምጽዋት ደስ ይብለኒ
1.17 ክላሲካዊ ትልሂት ደስ ይብለኒ
1.18 ብእግሪ ምዝዋር ደስ ይብለኒ

1.4 ኣብ ስፖርት ትሳተፍ ዲኻ፧

1.19 እወ፡ ኣብ በረኻ እጎዩ እየ
1.20 እወ፡ እዘልል እየ
1.21 እወ፡ እሕምብስ እየ
1.22 እወ፡ ኣብ ቅድድም ብሽክለታ እሳተፍ እየ
1.23 እወ፡ ኵዕሶ እግሪ እጻወት እየ
1.24 እወ፡ ተኒስ እጻወት እየ
1.25 እወ፡ ኵዕሶ ሰኪዐት እጻወት እየ
1.26 እወ፡ ናይ ኢድ ኩዕሶ እጻወት እየ
1.27 እወ፡ ራግቢ እጻወት እየ

1.11 Mi piace la fotografia.
1.12 Mi piace il modellismo.
1.13 Mi piace il computer.
1.14 Mi piace il calcio.
1.15 Mi piace la musica.
1.16 Mi piace suonare la chitarra.
1.17 Mi piace la danza classica.
1.18 Mi piace passeggiare.

1.4 Pratichi qualche sport?
Fai qualche sport?

1.19 Sì, faccio corsa campestre.
1.20 Sì, faccio salto in alto.
1.21 Sì, faccio nuoto.
1.22 Sì, faccio ciclismo.
1.23 Sì, gioco a calcio.
1.24 Sì, gioco a tennis.
1.25 Sì, gioco a pallacanestro.
1.26 Sì, gioco a pallamano.
1.27 Sì, gioco a rugby.

2.1 What do you usually do in the evening?
2.2 How do you spend your evenings?

2.7 I watch television.
2.8 I listen to music.
2.9 I go out with my friends.
2.10 I read a book.
2.11 I play cards.
2.12 Nothing in particular.

2.3 What do you like to read?

2.13 I like adventure books.
2.14 I like science fiction books
2.15 I like sports papers.
2.16 I like comics.
2.17 I like fashion magazines.
2.18 I like music magazines.

2.4 What kind of music do you prefer?

2.19 (I prefer) pop music.
2.20 (I prefer) classical music.
2.21 (I prefer) jazz.
2.22 (I prefer) folk music.

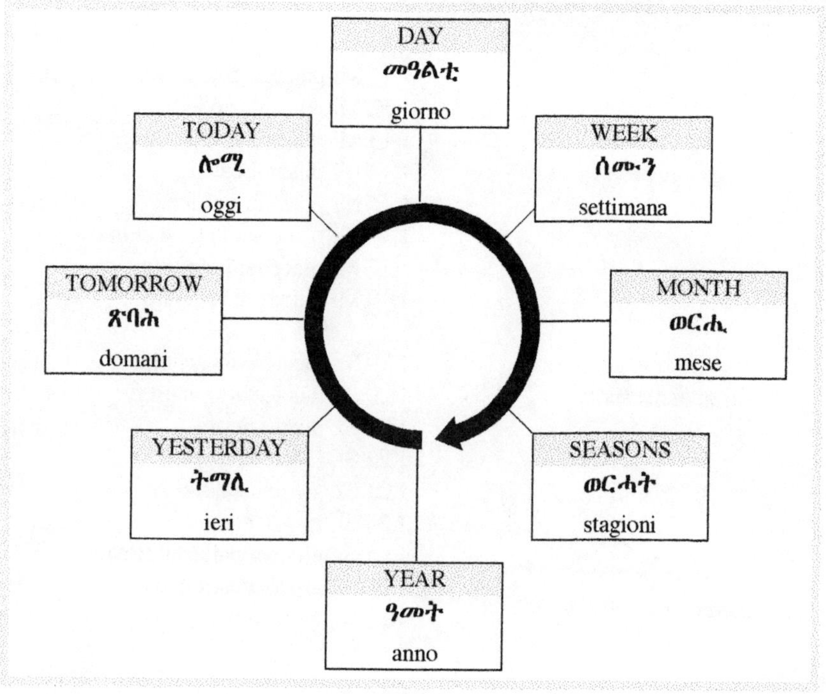

2.1 መብዛሕትኡ ግዜ ምሸት እንታይ ትገብር፧
2.2 ምሸት ከመይ ተሕልፎ፧

2.7 ተለቪዥን እርኢ.
2.8 ሙዚቃ እሰምዕ
2.9 ምስ ኣዕሩኽተይ እወጽእ
2.10 መጽሓፍ ኣንብብ
2.11 ካርታ እጻወት
2.12 ዋላ ሓደ ፍሉይ ነገር ኣይገብርን

2.3 እንታይ ምንባብ ደስ ይብለካ፧

2.13 ናይ ዕንደራ መጻሕፍቲ ደስ ይብለኒ
2.14 ናይ ሳይንስ ፊክሽን ምንባብ ደስ ይብለኒ
2.15 ናይ ስፖርት ጋዜጣታት ምንባብ ደስ ይብለኒ
2.16 ቶፖሊኖ ምንባብ ደስ ይብለኒ
2.17 ናይ ሞዳ መጽሔታት ምንባብ ደስ ይብለኒ
2.18 ናይ ሙዚቃ መጽሔታት ምንባብ ደስ ይብለኒ

2.4 እንታይ ዓይነት ሙዚቃ ትመርጽ፧

2.19 ፖፕ ሙዚቃ እመርጽ
2.20 ክላሲካል ሙዚቃ እመርጽ
2.21 ጃዝ ሙዚቃ እመርጽ
2.22 ባህላዊ ሙዚቃ እመርጽ

2.1 Che cosa fai di solito la sera?
2.2 Come passi le serate?

2.7 Guardo la televisione.
2.8 Ascolto musica.
2.9 Esco con gli amici.
2.10 Leggo qualche libro.
2.11 Gioco a carte.
2.12 Non faccio niente di particolare.

2.3 Che cosa ti piace leggere?

2.13 Mi piacciono i libri di avventura.
2.14 Mi piacciono i libri di fantascienza.
2.15 Mi piacciono i giornali sportivi.
2.16 Mi piacciono i fumetti.
2.17 Mi piacciono le riviste di moda.
2.18 Mi piacciono le riviste di musica.

2.4 Che tipo di musica preferisci?

2.19 (Preferisco) la musica pop.
2.20 (Preferisco) la musica classica.
2.21 (Preferisco) la musica jazz.
2.22 (Preferisco) la musica folk.

2.5 What do you do at weekends ?
2.6 What do you do during the holidays?

2.23 I sometimes go horse-riding.
2.24 I often go to play ...
2.25 I usually go dancing.
2.26 I usually go fishing.
2.27 I usually go to the theatre.
2.28 I usually go to see friends.
2.29 I usually go to the cinema.
2.30 I usually go to the sports club.
2.31 I usually go to concerts.
2.32 I usually go to discos.

3.1 Which television programmes do you prefer?
3.2 Which are your favourite programmes?

3.10 I like cartoons.
3.11 I like musical programmes.
3.12 I like plays.
3.13 I like documentaries on nature.
3.14 I like sports programmes.
3.15 I like current affairs programmes.
3.16 I like serials.

2.5 ቀዳመ ሰንበት እንታይ ትገብር፧
2.6 ኣብ ዕረፍቲ ግዜኻ እንታይ ትገብር፧

2.23 ሓደ ሓደ ግዜ ብፈረስ እዛወር
2.24 መብዛሕትኡ ግዜ ንኸጻወት ... እወጽእ
2.25 መብዛሕትኡ ግዜ ንኸስዕስዕ እወጽእ
2.26 መብዛሕትኡ ግዜ ዓሳ ንኸገፍፍ እወጽእ
2.27 መብዛሕትኡ ግዜ ትያትር እኸይድ
2.28 መብዛሕትኡ ግዜ ኣዕሩኽተይ ክረክብ እወጽእ
2.29 መብዛሕትኡ ግዜ ናብ ሲነማ እኸይድ
2.30 መብዛሕትኡ ግዜ ናብ ስፖርት ክበብ እኸይድ
2.31 መብዛሕትኡ ግዜ ናብ ኮንሰርት እኸይድ
2.32 መብዛሕትኡ ግዜ ናብ ዲስኮ እኸይድ

3.1 ኣየናይ ናይ ተለቪዥን ፕሮግራም ትመርጽ፧
3.2 ኣየናይ ናይ ተለቪዥን ፕሮግራም ደስ ይብለካ፧

3.10 ካርቱን ፊልም ደስ ይብለኒ
3.11 ናይ ሙዚቃ ፕሮግራም ደስ ይብለኒ
3.12 ተዋስኦ ደስ ይብለኒ
3.13 ደኩሜንታሪ ፊልም ደስ ይብለኒ
3.14 ናይ ስፖርት ፕሮግራም ደስ ይብለኒ
3.15 ናይ ዜና ፕሮግራም ደስ ይብለኒ
3.16 ናይ ፍቕሪ ፊልም ደስ ይብለኒ

2.5 Che cosa fai durante il fine settimana?
2.6 Che cosa fai durante le vacanze?

2.23 Qualche volta vado a cavallo.
2.24 Spesso vado a giocare a ...
2.25 Di solito vado a ballare.
2.26 Di solito vado a pescare.
2.27 Di solito vado a teatro.
2.28 Di solito vado a trovare gli amici.
2.29 Di solito vado al cinema.
2.30 Di solito vado al circolo sportivo.
2.31 Di solito vado ai concerti.
2.32 Di solito vado in discoteca.

3.1 Quali sono i programmi televisivi che preferisci?
3.2 Quali sono i tuoi programmi preferiti?

3.10 Mi piacciono i cartoni animati.
3.11 Mi piacciono i programmi musicali.
3.12 Mi piacciono le commedie.
3.13 Mi piacciono i documentari sulla natura.
3.14 Mi piacciono i programmi sportivi.
3.15 Mi piacciono i programmi di attualità.
3.16 Mi piacciono i teleromanzi.

3.3 Which kind of films do you like? 3.4 What kind of films do you like?	3.17 I like comedies. 3.18 I like westerns. 3.19 I like dramas. 3.20 I like adventure films. 3.21 I like romantic films. 3.22 I like historical films. 3.23 I like horror films.
3.5 Why?	3.24 Because they make me laugh. 3.25 Because they amuse me.
3.6 Did you like Fellini's film? 3.7 Did he like Goldoni's play? 3.8 Did she like the cartoons? 3.9 Did you like the songs ...?	3.26 I did/didn't like it. 3.27 He did/didn't like it. 3.28 She did/didn't like them. 3.29 We did/didn't like them.
4.1 (At) what time does the next show start? 4.2 (At) what time does the next show finish?	4.3 It starts at eight. 4.4 It finishes at half past nine.

3.3 እንታይ ዓይነት ፊልም ደስ ይብለካ/ኪ፧
3.4 ኣየናይ ዓይነት ፊልም ደስ ይብለካ/ኪ፧

3.17 መስሓቕ ፊልም ደስ ይብለኒ
3.18 ካውቦይ ፊልም ደስ ይብለኒ
3.19 ዘሕዝን ፊልም ደስ ይብለኒ
3.20 ናይ ዕንደራ ፊልም ደስ ይብለኒ
3.21 ናይ ፍቕሪ ፊልም ደስ ይብለኒ
3.22 ታሪኻዊ ፊልም ደስ ይብለኒ
3.23 ዘፍርሕ ፊልም ደስ ይብለኒ

3.5 ንምንታይ፧

3.24 ስለ ዘስሕቐኒ
3.25 ስለ ዘዘናግዓኒ

3.6 ናይ ፌሊኒ ፊልም ተፈቲዩካዶ፧
3.7 ናይ ጎልዶኒ ትያትር ተፈትዩዎዶ፧
3.8 ናይ ካርቱን ፊልም ተፈትዩዋዶ፧
3.9 እቲ ... ደርፍታት ተፈትዩኩምዶ፧

3.26 ፈትየዮ/ኣይተፈተወንን
3.27 ፈትዩዎ/ኣይተፈተዎን
3.28 ፈትያቶ/ኣይተፈተዋን
3.29 ፈቲናዮ/ኣይተፈተወናን

4.1 ዚቕጽል ምርኢት ሰዓት ክንደይ ይጅምር፧
4.2 ዚቕጽል ምርኢት ሰዓት ክንደይ ይውድእ፧

4.3 ሰዓት ሸሞንተ ይጅምር
4.4 ሰዓት ትሽዓተን ፈረቓን ይውድእ

3.3 Che tipo di film ti piace?
3.4 Quali film ti piacciono?

3.17 Mi piacciono i film comici.
3.18 Mi piacciono i film western.
3.19 Mi piacciono i film drammatici.
3.20 Mi piacciono i film avventurosi.
3.21 Mi piacciono i film romantici.
3.22 Mi piacciono i film storici.
3.23 Mi piacciono i film dell'orrore.

3.5 Perché?

3.24 Perché mi fanno ridere.
3.25 Perché mi divertono.

3.6 Ti è piaciuto il film di Fellini?
3.7 Gli è piaciuta la commedia di Goldoni?
3.8 Le sono piaciuti i cartoni animati?
3.9 Vi sono piaciute le canzoni ...?

3.26 (Non) mi è piaciuto.
3.27 (Non) gli è piaciuta.
3.28 (Non) le sono piaciuti.
3.29 (Non) ci sono piaciute.

4.1 A che ora inizia il prossimo spettacolo?
4.2 A che ora finisce il prossimo spettacolo?

4.3 Comincia alle otto.
4.4 Termina alle nove e mezzo.

14 EDUCATION AND FUTURE CAREER

HOW TO ...
1. Exchange information about your present school
2. Exchange information about when lessons begin and end
3. Exchange information about how many lessons there are and how long they last
4. Exchange information about homework
5. Exchange information about subjects studied
6. Exchange information about your plans for the future

1.1 What school do you attend?	1.10 I attend the ...
1.2 What year are you in?	1.11 The first (year). 1.12 The second (year).
1.3 What class are you in?	1.13 The third. 1.14 The fourth.

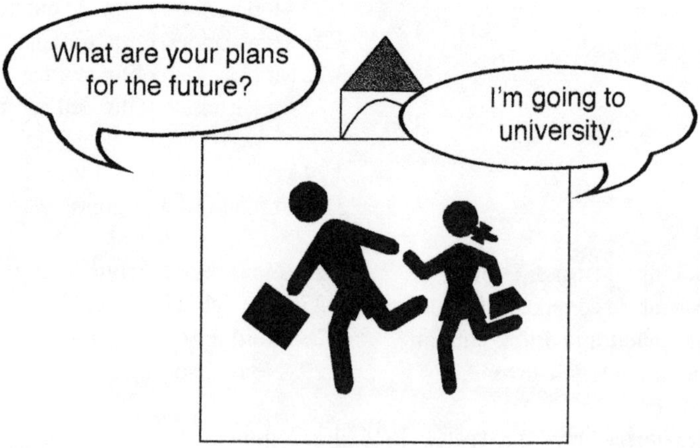

ትምህርትን ዕድል መጻኢ ስራሕን

ከመይ ጌርካ ...
1. ብዛዕባ እትመሃረሉ ቤት ትምህርቲ ሓበሬታ ከም እትለዋወጥ
2. ብዛዕባ ናይ ትምህርቲ ሰዓታትን ናቶም ንውሓትን ሓበሬታ ከም እትለዋወጥ
3. ብዛዕባ ክንደይ ዓይነት ትምህርቲ ከም ዘለዉን ክንደይ ግዜ ከም ዚወስዱን ሓበሬታ ከም እትለዋወጥ
4. ብዛዕባ ዕዮ ገዛ ሓበሬታ ከም እትለዋወጥ
5. ብዛዕባ እትመሃሮ ዓይነት ትምህርቲ ሓሳብ ከም እትለዋወጥ
6. ብዛዕባ ናይ መጻኢ መደብ ሓበሬታ ከም እትለዋወጥ

1.1 ኣበይ ትምሃር፧	1.10 ኣብ ... እምሃር
1.2 ኣብ ኣየናይ ክፍሊ (ዓመት) ትምሃር፧	1.11 ቀዳማይ (ዓመት) 1.12 ካልኣይ (ዓመት)
1.3 ኣብ ክንደይ ክፍሊ ኣሎኻ፧	1.13 ሳልሳይ 1.14 ራብዓይ

ISTRUZIONE E CARRIERA

Come ...
1. scambiarsi informazioni sulla scuola che si frequenta
2. scambiarsi informazioni sull'inizio e la fine delle lezioni
3. scambiarsi informazioni sulle ore di lezione e sulla loro durata
4. scambiarsi informazioni sui compiti
5. scambiarsi informazioni sulle materie studiate
6. scambiarsi informazioni sui propri programmi per il futuro

1.1 Che scuola frequenti?	1.10 Frequento ...
1.2 Che anno frequenti?	1.11 Il primo (anno). 1.12 Il secondo (anno).
1.3 Che classe fai?	1.13 La terza 1.14 La quarta

1.4 Where is your school?	1.17 It's in Rome Square. 1.18 It's in the centre.
1.5 Is your school big? 1.6 Is your school small?	1.19 It's quite large.
1.7 Are the classes large?	1.20 No, there are usually about twenty of us.
1.8 Is it a good school?	1.21 Yes, the teachers are very good. 1.22 No, it is lacking in facilities.
1.9 Are there many sports facilities?	1.23 There's a gymnasium. 1.24 There's a swimming pool. 1.25 There's a tennis court. 1.26 There's a volleyball court. 1.27 There's a basketball court.
2.1 At what time do the lessons start? 2.2 At what time do the lessons finish?	2.3 (They start) at eight. 2.4 (They finish) at one.

1.4 ቤት ትምህርትኻ ኣበይ ትርከብ፧

1.17 ኣብ ፒያሳ ሮማ
1.18 ኣብ ማእከል (ከተማ)

1.5 ቤት ትምህርትኻ ዓባይ ዲያ፧
1.6 ቤት ትምህርትኻ ንእሽተይ ዲያ፧

1.19 ብመጠኑ ዓባይ ኢያ

1.7 ብዙሓት ተመሃሮ ኣለዉዶ፧

1.20 ኣይፋልን፣ ዝበዝሕ ግዜ ኣስታት ዕስራ ኢና

1.8 ጥዑይ ቤት ትምህርቲ ዲዩ፧

1.21 እወ፣ እቶም መምህራን ኣዚዮም ንፉዓት ኢዮም
1.22 ኣይፋልን፣ ናይ መሳርሒታት ስእነት ኣለዎ

1.9 ብዙሕ ናይ ስፖርት መሳርሒ ኣሎዶ፧

1.23 ሓንቲ ናይ ስፖርት ክፍሊ ኣላ
1.24 ሓንቲ መሐንበሲት ኣላ
1.25 ሓደ ሜዳ ተኒስ ኣሎ
1.26 ሓደ ሜዳ ኩዕሶ መርበብ ኣሎ
1.27 ሓደ ሜዳ ኩዕሶ ሰኪዐት ኣሎ

2.1 ትምህርቲ ሰዓት ክንደይ ይጅምር፧
2.2 ትምህርቲ ሰዓት ክንደይ ይውዳእ፧

2.3 ሰዓት ሸሞንተ (ይጅምር)
2.4 ሰዓት ሓደ (ይውዳእ)

1.4 Dove si trova la tua scuola?

1.17 E' in Piazza Roma.
1.18 E' in centro.

1.5 E' una scuola grande?
1.6 E' una scuola piccola?

1.19 E' una scuola piccola.

1.7 Le classi sono numerose?

1.20 No, siamo in genere una ventina.

1.8 E' una buona scuola?

1.21 Sì, gli insegnanti sono molto bravi.
1.22 No, è carente di molte strutture.

1.9 Ci sono molte attrezzature sportive?

1.23 C'è una palestra.
1.24 C'è una piscina.
1.25 C'è un campo da tennis.
1.26 C'è un campo da pallavolo.
1.27 C'è un campo da pallacanestro.

2.1 A che ora iniziano le lezioni?
2.2 A che ora finiscono le lezioni?

2.3 (Iniziano) alle otto.
2.4 (Finiscono) alle tredici.

3.1 How many hours (of lessons) do you have?	3.4 (Usually) five hours.
3.2 How long does a lesson last?	3.5 One hour. 3.6 Fifty minutes.
4.1 Are you given much class-work? 4.2 Are you given much homework?	4.3 Too much! 4.4 Quite a lot! 4.5 Yes, mostly Mathematics, ...
5.1 What subjects do you study?	5.6 (I study) Italian and French. 5.7 (I study) English and Tigrinya. 5.8 (I study) German and Arabic. 5.9 (I study) Maths. 5.10 (I study) Science. 5.11 (I study) History. 5.12 (I study) Geography. 5.13 (I study) Art. 5.14 (I study) P.E. 5.15 (I study) Music.

3.1 ክንደይ ናይ ትምህርቲ ሰዓታት ኣለኩም፧

3.4 (ዝበዝሐ ግዜ) ሓሙሽተ ሰዓት

3.2 ሓንቲ ፐሬድ ክንደይ ትጸንሕ፧

3.5 ሓንቲ ሰዓት
3.6 ሓምሳ ደቒቕ

4.1 ብዙሕ ናይ ክፍሊ ዕዮ ይህቡኻ ዲዮም፧
4.2 ብዙሕ ናይ ገዛ ዕዮ ይህቡኻ ዲዮም፧

4.3 ኣዚዩ ብዙሕ
4.4 ብመጠኑ
4.5 እወ፡ ብፍላይ ናይ ሕሳብ ...

5.1 እንታይ ዓይነት ትምህርቲ ትምሃር፧

5.6 ጥልያንን ፈረንሳን (እምሃር)
5.7 እንግሊዝን ትግርኛን (እምሃር)
5.8 ጀርመንን ዓረብን (እምሃር)
5.9 ሕሳብ (እምሃር)
5.10 ስነ ፍልጠት (እምሃር)
5.11 ታሪኽ (እምሃር)
5.12 ጂኦግራፊ (እምሃር)
5.13 ስእሊ (እምሃር)
5.14 ስፖርት (እምሃር)
5.15 ሙዚቃ (እምሃር)

3.1 Quante ore di lezione avete?

3.4 (Di solito) cinque ore.

3.2 Quanto dura una lezione?

3.5 Un'ora.
3.6 Cinquanta minuti.

4.1 Ti danno molti compiti in classe?
4.2 Ti danno molti compiti a casa?

4.3 Troppi!
4.4 Abbastanza!
4.5 Sì, soprattutto di matematica.

5.1 Che materie studi?

5.6 (Studio) italiano e francese.
5.7 (Studio) inglese e tigrino.
5.8 (Studio) tedesco e arabo
5.9 (Studio) matematica.
5.10 (Studio) scienze.
5.11 (Studio) storia.
5.12 (Studio) geografia.
5.13 (Studio) educazione artistica.
5.14 (Studio) educazione fisica.
5.15 (Studio) educazione musicale.

5.2 What's your favourite subject? 5.3 Which are your favourite subjects?	
5.4 Do you like Mathematics? 5.5 Do you like Literature?	5.17 Yes, I do/I like it. 5.18 No, I don't (like it).
6.1 What are your plans for the future?	6.4 I am going to university. 6.5 I am going to work.
6.2 What will you do when you have finished school?	6.7 I will look for a job. 6.8 I am going to France for a year. 6.9 (I don't know) we'll see ...
6.3 What kind of work would you like to do?	6.10 I would like to be an architect. 6.11 I would like to be a journalist. 6.12 I would like to be a hairdresser. 6.13 I would like to be a mechanic. 6.14 I would like to be a teacher.

5.2 ኣየናይ ዓይነት ትምህርቲ ደስ ይብለካ፧
5.3 ኣየኖት ዓይነታት ትምህርቲ ደስ ይብሉኻ፧

5.4 ቍጽሪ ትፈቱዶ፧
5.5 ስነጽሑፍ ትፈቱዶ፧

5.17 እወ፡ ይፍተወኒ ኢዩ
5.18 ኣይፋልን፡ ኣይፍተወንን ኢዩ

6.1 ናይ መጻኢ መደባትካ እንታይ ኢዩ፧

6.4 ዩኒቨርሲቲ ክመሃር እየ
6.5 ስራሕ ክጅምር እየ

6.2 ትምህርቲ ምስ ወዳእካ እንታይ ክትገብር ኢኻ፧

6.7 ስራሕ ክደሊ እየ
6.8 ንሓደ ዓመት ንዓዲ ፈረንሳ ክኸይድ እየ
6.9 (ኣይፈለጥኩን) ንርእዮ ...

6.3 እንታይ ዓይነት ስራሕ ምስራሕ ደስ ምበለካ፧

6.10 ሃናጺ ምኾንኩ ደስ ምበለኒ
6.11 ጋዜጠኛ ምኾንኩ ደስ ምበለኒ
6.12 መሻጢ ምኾንኩ ደስ ምበለኒ
6.13 መካኒክ ምኾንኩ ደስ ምበለኒ
6.14 መምህር ምኾንኩ ደስ ምበለኒ

5.2 Qual è la tua materia preferita?
5.3 Quali sono le tue materie preferite?

5.4 Ti piace la matematica?
5.5 Ti piace la letteratura?

5.17 Sì, mi piace.
5.18 No, non mi piace ...

6.1 Quali sono i tuoi progetti per il futuro?

6.4 Andrò all'università.
6.5 Andrò a lavorare.

6.2 Che cosa farai, quando avrai finito la scuola?

6.7 Cercherò un impiego.
6.8 Andrò un anno in Francia.
6.9 (Non lo so) vedremo ...

6.3 Che lavoro ti piacerebbe fare?

6.10 Mi piacerebbe fare l'architetto.
6.11 Mi piacerebbe fare il giornalista.
6.12 Mi piacerebbe fare il parrucchiere.
6.13 Mi piacerebbe fare il meccanico.
6.14 Mi piacerebbe fare l'insegnante.

15 LANGUAGE FUNCTIONS

1. Greeting People

1. Hello!, Hi.
2. Hello!
3. Good morning!/
   Good afternoon!

4. Good morning, Mr./Mrs/Miss

5. Good evening ...

2. Introducing Someone And Being Introduced

1. This is ...
2. This is Mr...
3. May I introduce Mr... (to you?)

4. My name is ...
5. Hallo! (I am Carla).
6. How do you do?
7. Pleased to meet you!

3. Taking Leave

1. Bye!
2. See you soon!
3. Goodbye!

4. Good night!
5. See you later!
6. See you tomorrow!

1. ሰላምታ ምልውዋጥ

1. ቻው
2. ሰላማት
3. ከመይ ውዒልካ/ኩም፣ ከመይ ውዒልኪ/ክን
4. ከመይ ውዒልካ/ኪ ኣቶ/ ወይዘሮ/ወይዘሪት
5. ደሓን ኣምሲ/ዩ፣ ኣምስዪ/ያ...

1. Salutare

1. Ciao!
2. Salve!
3. Buongiorno!
4. Buongiorno, signor/signora/signorina ...
5. Buonasera ...

2. ንሰብ ምልላይን ንነብስኻ ምልላይን

1. እዚ/ እዚኣ ... ኢ.ያ/ዩ
2. ኣቶ ... ይብሃሉ
3. ምስ ኣቶ ... ከላልየካዶ፧
4. ስመይ ... ይብሃል
5. ቻው (ካርላ እብሃል)
6. ከመይ ኣሎኻ/ኺ
7. ጽቡቕ ሌላ ይግበረልና

2. Presentare qualcuno e presentarsi

1. Questo/questa è ...
2. Le presento il signor ...*
3. Posso presentarle il signor ... *
4. Mi chiamo ...
5. Ciao, (io sono Carla).
6. Piacere!
7. Molto lieto!

3. ምብጋስ

1. ደሓን ኩን/ኩኑ/ኩኒ/ኩና
2. ብደሓን የራኽበና
3. ደሓን ኩን/ኒ
4. ደሓን ሕደር/ሪ
5. ክንራኸብ ኢ.ና
6. ጽባሕ የራኽበና

3. Congedarsi

1. Ciao!
2. (Ciao), a presto!
3. Arrivederci!
3.1. ArrivederLa! *
4. Buonanotte!
5. A più tardi!
6. A domani!

* FORMALE

4. Attracting Attention

1. Excuse me ...
2. Excuse me, please ...

5. Congratulating

1. Well done!
2. Congratulations!
3. You've done very well!

6. Expressing Good Wishes

1. Best wishes!
2. All the best!
3. I wish you ...
4. Merry Christmas!
5. Happy New Year!
6. Happy Easter!
7. Happy Birthday!
8. Have a good holiday!
9. Have a good trip!

7. Expressing And Responding To Thanks

1. Thanks!
2. Thanks a lot/ thank you very much!
3. Thank you for ...
4. Thank you!
5. I don't know how to thank you!
6. Don't mention it!
7. It's all right!
8. It has been a pleasure!

4. ኣቓልቦ ምስሓብ

1. ይቕረታ ...
2. ብኽብረትካ/ኩም/ኪ/ክን ...

4. Richiamare l'attenzione

1. Scusa ...
   (Mi) scusi ... *
2. Senta, per favore ... *

5. ምትብባዕ

1. ኮርዒዳ
2. እንቋዕ ልብኻ ሓጒሰካ
3. ኣሓጒስካና/ኣሓጒስኩምና/ኣሓጒስክና/ኣሓጒስክናና

5. Congratularsi

1. Bravo!
2. Congratulazioni!
3. Sei stato bravissimo!

6. እንቋዕ ሓጐሰካ/ኩም/ኪ/ክን

1. ሰናይ ምንዮት
2. ኩሉ ጽቡቕ ዘበለ እምነየልካ/ኪ
3. ... እምነየልካ/ኪ
4. ርሑስ ልደት
5. ርሑስ ሓዲሽ ዓመት
6. ርሑስ ፋስጋ
7. ጽቡቕ ልደት
8. ጽቡቕ ዕረፍቲ
9. ጽቡቕ መገሻ

6. Augurare

1. Auguri!
2. I migliori auguri!
3. Ti auguro ...
   Le auguro ...*
4. Buon Natale!
5. Buon Anno!
6. Buona Pasqua!
7. Buon compleanno!
8. Buone vacanze!
9. Buon viaggio!

7. መልሲ ንምስጋና

1. የቐንየለይ
2. ብዙሕ የቐንየለይ
3. የቐንየለይ በቲ ...
4. እመስግን
5. ከመይ ገይረ ከም ዘመስግነካ/ኪ ኣይፈልጥን
6. ገንዘብካ/ኩም/ኪ/ክን
7. ምንም ኣይኮነን
8. ብሓቂ ዘሐጐስ ኢዩ

7. Ringraziare e rispondere ai ringraziamenti

1. Grazie!
2. Grazie mille!
3. Grazie per ...
4. Ti ringrazio!/La ringrazio!*
5. Non so come ringraziarti!
   Non so come ringraziarLa! *
6. Prego!
7. Di niente!
8. E' stato un piacere!

8. Expressing Lack Of Understanding

1. Pardon?
2. (I beg your) pardon?

3./4. I don't understand.
5. I haven't understood.

6. Would you repeat it, please?
7. What does it mean?
8. Can you repeat it, please?
9. It is not clear.

9. Expressing Agreement And Disagreement

1. I agree.
2. You're right!
3. Of course!
4. Right!

5. I don't agree!
6. You are wrong!
7. It's not true!
8. Not at all!

10. Expressing Surprise

1. What a surprise!
2. What a nice surprise!
3. This is a real surprise!
4. No kidding?
5. I can't believe it!
6. No!

8. ዘይምርድዳእ

1. እንታይ፧ ይቕሬታ፧
2. ይቕሬታ፡ እንታይ በልኩም/ክን፧

3. ይቕሬታ፡ ኣይተረደኣንን
4. ኣይተረደኣንን
5. ኣይተረደኣንን

6. በጃኹም ድገሙለይ
7. እንታይ ማለት ኢዩ
8. በጃኻ ድገመለይ
9. ብሩህ ኣይኮነን

8. Esprimere mancanza di comprensione e chiedere chiarimenti

1. Come, (scusa)?
2. Scusi, come ha detto? *

3. Prego? (Non ho capito!)
4. Non capisco.
5. Non ho capito.

6. Vuole ripetere, prego? *
7. Che cosa vuol dire?
8. Puoi ripetere, per favore?
9. Non è chiaro.

9. ምስምማዕ፡ ዘይምስምማዕ

1. እሰማማዕ'የ
2. ጽቡቕ ኣሎኻ/ኺ
3. ርዱእ
4. ልክዕ

5. ኣይሰማማዕን'የ
6. ትጋገ ኣሎኻ/ኺ
7. ሓሶት
8. ብጥራሽ

9. Esprimere accordo e disaccordo

1. Sono d'accordo.
2. Hai (proprio) ragione!
3. Naturalmente!
4. Giusto!

5. Non sono d'accordo!
6. Sbagli!
7. Non è vero!
8. Per niente!

10. ምግራም

1. ዘገርም'ዩ
2. እነሀልካ በል ንብስራት
3. ዘደንጽ ኢዩ
4. ቁም ነገር፧
5. ኣይኣምንን
6. ኣይፋልን/ኣይከውንን

10. Esprimere sorpresa

1. Che sorpresa!
2. Che bella sorpresa!
3. Questa sì che è una sorpresa!
4. Davvero!
5. Non ci credo!
6. No!

11. Expressing Hope

1. Let's hope so!
2. I hope so!
3. If only!
4. I hope you'll be better.

12. Expressing Satisfaction

1. Wonderful!
2. How lovely!
3. I'm very happy/satisfied ...
4. It's just what I wanted.
5. It's lovely!

13. Expressing Gratitude

1. I am very grateful to you ...
2. You've been very kind S...
3. Thank you!
4. Thanks for everything!

14. Apologizing

1. Sorry!
2. I am so sorry!
3. I apologize for ...
4. I am sorry!

11. ተስፋ ምግላጽ

1. ተስፋ ንገብር
2. ምሉእ ተስፋ ኣሎና
3. ይግበረልና
4. ጽቡቕ ክትህሉ/ልዊ ተስፋ ንገብር

11. Esprimere speranza

1. Speriamo!
2. Speriamo di sì.
3. Magari!
4. Speriamo che tu stia meglio!

12. ዕግበት ምግላጽ

1. ግሩም
2. ኣየ ክጽብቕ
3. … ዕጉብ'የ
4. ክምኡ'የ ደልየ ነይረ
5. ኣዚዩ ጽቡቕ'ዩ

12. Esprimere soddisfazione

1. Magnifico!
2. Che bello!
3. Sono contento/soddisfatto ...
4. E' proprio quello che desideravo.
5. E' molto bello!

13. ምስጋና ምግላጽ

1. … ኣዚየ አመስግነካ/ኪ
2. … ኣዚየ አመስግነኩም/ክን
3. የቐንየለይ
4. ኣብ ካሕሳኻ/ኺ የውዕለኒ

13. Esprimere gratitudine

1. Ti sono molto grato ...
   Le sono molto grato ... *
2. Sei stato molto gentile ...
   E' stato molto gentile ... *
3. La ringrazio! *
4. Grazie di tutto!

14. ይቕረታ ምሕታት

1. ይቕረታ
2. በጃኻ/ኺ ኣይትሓዘለይ/ዝለይ
3. … ይቕረታ እሓትት
4. ኣይትሓዘለይ

14. Chiedere scusa

1. Scusa!
   Scusi! *
2. Scusami (tanto)!
3. Mi scuso per ...
4. Mi dispiace!

15. Expressing Indifference

1. I don't care!
2. It's all the same to me.
3. Do as you like!

16. Suggesting A Course Of Action (Including The Speaker)

1. Shall we go ...?
2. We could ...
3. Will you come with us ...?
4. Would you like to ...?

17. Requesting Others To Do Something

1. Could you ...?
2. Would you mind ...?
3. I would be very grateful if you could ...

18. Asking For Advice

1. What do you think of ...?
2. Any ideas?
3. What would you do (in my situation?)
4. What do you suggest?
5. What would you suggest?

15. ግዳስ ዘይምርኣይ

1. ኣይግድሰንን'ዩ
2. ንዓይ ኩሉ ሓደ'ዩ
3. ከም ድልየትካ/ኪ ግበር/ሪ

15. Esprimere indifferenza

1. Non mi interessa!
2. Per me è lo stesso.
3. Fai come vuoi!

16. ብዛዕባ ገለ ተግባራት ሓሳብ ምቕራብ

1. ንኺድዶ፧
2. ... ምኽኣልና
3. ምሳና ትኽይድዶ/ትኽዲዶ፧
4. ... ደስ ምበለካዶ
   ደስ ምበለኩምዶ/ምበለክንዶ፧

16. Proporre

1. Andiamo ...?
2. Potremmo ...
3. Vieni con noi ...?
4. Ti andrebbe di ...?
   Le andrebbe di ... ? *

17. ካልኦት ገለ ስራሕ ንኺገብሩ ምውካስ

1. ምኽኣልካዶ ምኽኣልኩምዶ/
   ምኽኣልክንዶ ... ፧
2. ደስዶ ምበለካ/ኪ ደስዶ
   ምበለኩም/ክን ... ፧
3. ... ክትግብሩ/ራ እንተ
   ትኽእላ መመስገንኩኹም/ኹን

17. Chiedere di fare qualcosa

1. Potresti ...?
   Potrebbe ...? *
2. Ti spiacerebbe ...?
   Le spiacerebbe ...? *
3. Le sarei molto grato se potesse ...

18. ምኽሪ ምሕታት

1. እንታይ ይመስለካ/ኪ ... ፧
2. ገለ ሓሳባት ኣሎካ/ኪዶ፧
3. (ኣብ ቦታይ እንተ ትነብር/ሪ) እንታይ
   ምገበርካ/ኪ፧
4. እንታይ ሓሳብ ምሃብካኒ/ክኒ
5. እንታይ ሓሳብ ምሃብክሙኒ/ናኒ

18. Chiedere un parere

1. Che ne pensi ...?
2. Hai qualche idea?
3. Che cosa faresti
   (al mio posto)?
4. Che cosa mi consigli?
5. Che cosa mi consiglia?*

GRAMMAR REVIEW

UNIT 1 PERSONAL IDENTIFICATION

What's What is	your name?

(My name is) I'm	Mary. Charles.

Are	you you they	from	Eritrea? England? Italy?
Is	he she		

Yes,	I am. we are. they are. he is. she is.

No,	I'm not. we aren't. they aren't. he isn't. she isn't.

Are	you you they	Eritrean? English? Italian?
Is	he she	

No,	I'm we're they're he's she's	French. Australian. American.

Do	you you they	like	Italian? this book? this pen?
Does	he she		

Yes,	I we they	like	it.
	he she	likes	

UNITÀ 1 IDENTIFICAZIONE PERSONALE

Come	ti chiami?

(Mi chiamo)	Maria. Carlo.

Vieni Venite Vengono Viene	(tu) (voi) (loro) (lui/lei)	dall'	Eritrea? Inghilterra? Italia?

Sì, No,	(io) vengo (noi) veniamo (loro) vengono (lui/lei) viene	dall'	Eritrea.

Sei	(tu)	eritreo?
Siete	(voi)	inglesi?
Sono	(loro)	italiani?
E'	(lui)	italiano?
E'	(lei)	italiana?

No,	(io)	sono	francese.
	(noi)	siamo	australiani.
	(loro)	sono	americani.
	(lui)	è	americano.
	(lei)	è	americana.

Ti Vi Gli Gli Le	piace	l'italiano? questo libro? questa penna?

Sì,	mi ci gli gli le	piace.

UNIT 2 FAMILY

What's	your	father grandfather brother uncle cousin son husband mother grandmother sister aunt cousin daughter wife	called?
	his/her name?		

He's She's	called ...
His/Her name's ...	

What job	does	your	father mother	do?
	do		you	

He's She's I'm	an architect. a teacher. unemployed.

Do	you you they	have	any pets at home?
Does	he/she		

Yes,	I we they	have	a	cat. dog.
	he/she	has		

UNITÀ 2 FAMIGLIA

Come si chiama	tuo	padre? nonno? fratello? zio? cugino? figlio? marito?
	tua	madre? nonna? sorella? zia? cugina? figlia? moglie?

Si	chiama ...

Che lavoro	fa	tuo padre? tua madre?
	fai?	

E'	architetto. maestro/a.
Sono	disoccupato/a.

Hai Avete Hanno Ha	animali in casa?

Sì,	ho abbiamo hanno ha	un	gatto. cane.

UNIT 3 HOUSE AND HOME

Where	do	you you they	live?
	does	he she	

I we they	live	in	the town-centre. a flat. a block of flats. a villa.
he she	lives		

Is there	central heating? a lift? a garden? a garage?

Yes,	there	is.
No,		isn't.

Where's (where is)	the	bathroom? toilet? pillow? blanket? cutlery?
Where are		plates?

Here	it is.
	they are.

What time do you	wake up? get up? have breakfast? have lunch? have dinner? go to bed?

I	wake up get up have breakfast have lunch have dinner go to bed	at ...

UNITÀ 3 CASA

Dove	abiti? abitate? abitano? abita (lui)? abita (lei)?

Abito Abitiamo Abitano Abita Abita	in	centro. un appartamento. un palazzo. una villa.

C'è	il riscaldamento centrale? l'ascensore? il giardino? il garage?

Sì,	c'è.
No, non	

Dove	è	il bagno? il gabinetto? il cuscino? la coperta?
	sono	le posate? i piatti?

Eccolo.
Eccola.
Eccole. Eccoli.

A che ora	ti	svegli? alzi?
	fai colazione? pranzi? ceni? vai a letto?	

Mi	sveglio alzo	alle ...
Faccio colazione Pranzo Ceno Vado a letto		

UNIT 4a GEOGRAPHICAL SURROUNDINGS

Where do you live?	I live	in	Eritrea. Italy. England. Rome. London. Chicago.

Where are you from?	I'm	from	Massawa. Ady Keyh.

Where is it?	It's	in	northern central southern the north of the south of	Eritrea.

Which is	the nearest	city?	It's	near	Massawa. London.

What's the countryside like?	It's	hilly. enchanting. monotonous. picturesque. wonderful.

Is	there	an	airport?	Yes,	there	is ...
		a	sports centre?	No,		isn't ...
Are		many	monuments?	Yes,		are ...
			industries?	No,		aren't ...

UNITÀ 4a AMBIENTE GEOGRAFICO

Dove vivi?

Vivo	in	Eritrea. Italia. Inghilterra.
	a	Roma. Londra. Chicago.

Di dove sei?

Sono	di	Massaua. Ady Keyh.

Dove si trova?

Si trova	nell' Eritrea		settentrionale. meridionale. centrale.
	nel	nord sud	Eritrea.

Qual è la città più vicina?

E'	vicina	a	Massawa. Londra.

Com'è il paesaggio?

E'	collinare. incantevole. monotono. pittoresco. stupendo.

C'è		un aeroporto? un centro sportivo?
Ci sono	molti	monumenti?
	molte	industrie?

Sì, No, non	c'è ...
Sì, No, non	ci sono ...

UNIT 4b WEATHER

What's the weather like?	It's	fine. bad. hot. cold. cool. raining. snowing. hailing. thundering. sunny. frosty. stormy. windy. foggy. misty.		
		a	fine bad	day.
	It is/The sky is	cloudy. overcast. dark. clear.		

What's the sea like today?	It's	calm. choppy. rough. very rough.

What's the climate like in	Germany? Italy? Spain? Eritrea?	It's a	continental mediterranean mild splendid	climate.

MONTHS	January, February, March, April, May, June, July, August, September, October, November, December.
SEASONS	Spring, Summer, Autumn, Winter.

UNITÀ 4b TEMPO ATMOSFERICO

Che tempo fa?	Fa bel tempo. brutto tempo. caldo. freddo. fresco.
	Piove. Nevica. Grandina. Tuona.
	C'è il sole. (il) ghiaccio. (il) temporale. vento. nebbia. foschia.
	E' una bella / brutta giornata.
	(Il cielo) è nuvoloso. coperto. scuro. sereno.

Com'è il mare oggi?	E' calmo. poco mosso. molto mosso. agitato.

Com'è il clima in	Germania? Italia? Spagna? Eritrea?	E' un clima	continentale. mediterraneo. mite. magnifico.

MESI	gennaio, febbraio, marzo, aprile, maggio, giugno, luglio, agosto, settembre, ottobre, novembre, dicembre.
STAGIONI	primavera, estate, autunno, inverno.

UNIT 5 TRAVEL AND TRANSPORT

Where's the	bus stop? station? information centre?

Take the	first second	on the	left. right.
Turn			
It's there, on your			
(Go) straight on.			
Go as far as the	traffic lights. cross-road.		
Cross the road.			

Is there	a	coach bus train	for	Florence?

Yes, there's one	in half an hour. at ten past seven.

What time does	it	leave get to	London? Oxford?

It	leaves gets in	at 3.00 p.m.

I'd like	a	single return	ticket	to	Rome.

At what time	are	you you they	leaving?
	is	he she	

I'm We're They're He's She'	leaving	at	six. seven. eight. nine. ten.

Can you check the	oil, water, tyres,	please?

UNITÀ 5 TRASPORTI

Dov'è	la fermata dell'autobus? la stazione? l'ufficio informazioni?

Prenda la	prima seconda	a	sinistra. destra.
Volti/giri			
E' lì sulla			
Continui Vada	sempre dritto. fino al semaforo. fino all'incrocio.		
Cross the road.			

C'è	una corriera un'autobus un treno	per	Firenze?

Sì, ce n'è uno	tra mezz'ora. alle sette e dieci.

A che ora	parte da arriva a	Londra? Oxford?

Parte Arriva	alle	15.00.

Vorrei	un	biglietto	di	andata andata e ritorno	per Roma.

A che ora	partirai (tu)? partirete (voi)? partiranno (loro)? partirà (lui)? partirà (lei)?

(Io) partirò (Noi) partiremo (Loro) partiranno (Lui) partirà (Lei) partirà	alle	sei. sette. otto. nove. dieci.

Mi controlli	l'olio, l'acqua, le gomme,	per favore?

UNIT 6-7 HOLIDAYS

Where do you	usually	go on holiday? spend your holidays?

Usually Often Sometimes	I go to	Eritrea. the mountains. the seaside.

Where	are	you you they	going on holiday?
	is	he she	

I'm We're They're	going to staying in	Florence.
He's She's		

Where would you like to go on holiday?

I'd like I would like	to go	to	Italy. America. Venice. Paris.

What do you usually do on holiday?

I go	skiing. to the seaside. for walks.
I do some sport.	

You We	could go to	the museum. the cinema. the theatre

Yes, that's a great idea.	
No,	I'm tired ... I'm busy ...

UNITÀ 6-7 VACANZE

Dove	vai	di solito	in vacanza?
	passi		le vacanze?

Di solito Spesso Qualche volta	vado	in Eritrea. in montagna. al mare.

Dove	andrai andrete andranno	in vacanza?
	andrà andrà	

Andrò Andremo Andranno	a Firenze. in Inghilterra.
Andrà Andrà	
Resterò	

Dove ti piacerebbe andare in vacanza?

Mi piacerebbe andare	in	Italia. America.
	a	Venezia. Parigi.

Che cosa fai di solito in vacanza?

Vado	a sciare. al mare.
Faccio delle passeggiate.	
Pratico qualche sport.	

Potresti Potremmo	andare	al museo. al cinema. a teatro.

Sì, è un'ottima idea.	
No,	sono stanco.... sono impegnato ...

UNIT 8 HOTEL

I have a room I haven't	booked.

Do you have	a	single double	room?

For	one night. two weeks. three days.

With Without	(a) bathroom. (a) shower.

How much is it	for one	night? person? room?

Could I see a room	on the first floor? with a view of the sea? at the front? at the back?

At what time is	breakfast lunch dinner	served?

UNITÀ 8 ALBERGHI

Ho una camera prenotata. Non ho prenotato.	

Avete una camera	singola? doppia?

Per	una notte. due settimane. tre giorni.

Con Senza	bagno. doccia.

Qual è il prezzo	per una	notte? persona? camera?

Potrei vedere una camera	al primo piano? con vista sul mare? sul davanti? sul retro?

A che ora servite	la prima colazione? il pranzo? la cena?

UNIT 9 FOOD AND DRINK

I'd like	a	coffee. cappuccino. sandwich. cheese roll.
	an	orangeade.

Do you have	(any)	ice-cream? cheese? fresh fruit?

Do you like	Italian Greek French Chinese Indian	cooking?

At what time do you have	breakfast? lunch? supper?

Could you please	bring me	some bread? the salt? the pepper? the tooth-picks?

UNITÀ 9 CIBI E BEVANDE

Vorrei	un	caffè. cappuccino. tramezzino. panino al formaggio.
	un'aranciata.	

Avete	del dolce? del formaggio? della frutta fresca?

Ti piace	la cucina	italiana? greca? francese? cinese? indiana?

A che ora fai	colazione? pranzi? ceni?

Mi porta	un po' di pane il sale il pepe gli stuzzicadenti	per favore?

UNIT 10 SHOPPING

Is there	a	supermarket? shopping centre? market? chemist's? butcher's? baker's?

Where's	the	food stationery clothing	department?

I'd like a	litre	of milk.
	kilo	of bread.
	dozen	eggs.
	box	of matches.
	plastic	bag.
	bottle	of wine.
	can	of orangeade.
	100 grams	of cheese.

I'd like	a pullover. a raincoat. an umbrella. a bag. a jacket.

Made of	nylon. leather. plastic. china. silk. metal. cotton.

UNITÀ 10 COMPERARE

C'è	un	supermercato? centro commerciale? mercato?
	una	farmacia? macelleria? panetteria?

Dov'è	il reparto	alimentari? cancelleria? vestiti/abbigliamento?

Vorrei	un litro	di latte.
	un chilo	di pane.
	una dozzina	di uova.
	una scatola	di fiammiferi.
	un sacchetto	di plastica.
	una bottiglia	di vino.
	una lattina	di aranciata.
	un etto	di formaggio.

Vorrei	un pullover. un impermeabile. un ombrello. una borsa. una giacca.

Di	nylon. pelle. plastica. porcellana. seta. metallo. cotone.

UNIT 11 SERVICES

How much is it to send	a	letter card parcel	to	Germany? America? Italy?

What stamp do I have to put	for	France? Great Britain? Australia?

I'd like to change	some travellers' cheques. Francs. Lire. Dollars.

What is the exchange rate for the	Pound? Deutsche Mark? French Franc? Dutch Guilder? Swiss Franc? U.S. Dollar? Australian Dollar? Canadian Dollar? Yen? Birr? Nakfa?

I've had	my	car camera	stolen ...

I have lost	my	bag. wallet.

UNITÀ 11 SERVIZI

Quanto costa spedire	una lettera una cartolina un pacco	in	Germania? America? Italia?

Che fracobollo devo mettere	per	la Francia? la Gran Bretagna? l'Australia?

Vorrei cambiare	dei travellers' cheque. dei franchi. delle lire. dei dollari.

Quant'è il cambio Qual è la quotazione	della sterlina? del marco tedesco? del franco francese? del fiorino olandese? del franco svizzero? del dollaro USA? del dollaro australiano? del dollaro canadese? dello yen? del birr? del nakfa?

Mi hanno rubato	la macchina/l'automobile. la macchina fotografica.

Ho perso	la borsa. il portafoglio.

UNIT 12 HEALTH

What's	wrong with you? wrong?
What How	do you feel?

I feel	weak. tired.
I've got	tooth ache. a sore throat. stomach-ache. back-ache. a head-ache. cramp. sun-stroke. diarrhoea. hay-fever. flu. high/low blood pressure.

I've	burnt hurt injured cut	myself.

I need I would like	to lie down. to go to bed. to see a doctor.

I would like	some	aspirin. plasters. tablets for ...

UNITÀ 12 SALUTE

Che cos'hai? Cos'è che non va? Che disturbo sente?* Come ti senti?

Mi sento		debole. stanco/a.
Ho	mal di	denti. gola. pancia. schiena. testa.
	i crampi. preso un colpo di sole. la diarrea. il raffreddore da fieno. l'influenza. la pressione alta/bassa.	

Mi sono	bruciato/a. fatto/a male. ferito/a. tagliato/a.

Ho bisogno di Vorrei	distendermi. coricarmi. un dottore/medico.

Vorrei	delle aspirine. dei cerotti. delle compresse di ...

UNIT 13 FREE TIME

What's your (favourite)	hobby?
What do you do in your	free time?

(I like)	collecting	stamps. post cards. stickers.
	playing	draughts. chess. cards. billiards.
		photography. electronics. model making. computers. football. music.

What do you do	at weekends? during the holidays?

I	usually sometimes often	go	dancing. horse-riding. to play ... fishing. to the theatre. to the cinema. to discos.

I	go	swimming. cycling. ice-skating.
	play	football. tennis. basket-ball.

UNITÀ 13 TEMPO LIBERO

Qual è il tuo hobby preferito? Che cosa fai nel tempo libero?

Mi piace	collezionare	francobolli. cartoline. adesivi.
	giocare a	dama. scacchi. carte. biliardo.
	la fotografia. l'elettronica. il modellismo. il computer. il calcio. la musica.	

Che cosa fai durante	il fine settimana? le vacanze?

Di solito Qualche volta Spesso	vado	a	ballare. cavallo. a giocare. pescare. teatro.
		al in	cinema. discoteca.

Faccio	nuoto. ciclismo. pattinaggio su ghiaccio.
Gioco a	calcio. tennis. pallacanestro.

UNIT 14 EDUCATION

What year are you in?	The	first second third fourth fifth	(year).

What subjects do you study?	(I study)	Arabic. French. German. English. Tigrinya. Italian. Maths. Science. History. Geography. Religion. Art. P.E. Music.

Do you like	Mathematics? Geography? Literature?	Yes, I like it. No, I don't like it. I prefer ...

What kind of work would you like to do?	I would like to be	an architect. a journalist. a hairdresser. a mechanic. a teacher.

UNITÀ 14 ISTRUZIONE

Che anno frequenti?	Il	primo secondo terzo quarto quinto	(anno).

Che materie studi?	(Studio)	arabo. francese. tedesco. inglese. tigrino. italiano. matematica. scienze. storia. geografia. religione. educazione artistica. educazione fisica. musica.

Ti piace la	matematica? geografia? letteratura?	Sì, mi piace. No, non mi piace. Preferisco ...

Che lavoro ti piacerebbe fare?	Mi piacerebbe fare	l'architetto. il giornalista. il parrucchiere. il meccanico. l'insegnante.

VOCABULARY LISTS BY TOPIC

PERSONAL IDENTIFICATION

Nationality

America	America	ኣመሪካ
americano	American	ኣመሪካዊ/ት
Africa	Africa	ኣፍሪቃ
Africano	African	ኣፍሪቃዊ/ት
Australia	Australia	ኦስትራሊያ
australiano	Australian	ኦስትራሊያዊ/ት
bandiera	flag	ባንዴራ
belga	Belgian	በልጂካዊ/ት
Belgio	Belgium	በልጂዩም
britannico	British	ብሪጣንያዊ/ት
carta di identità	identity card	ወረቐት መንነት
danese	Danish	ደንማርካዊ/ት
Danimarca	Denmark	ደንማርክ
Eritrea	Eritrea	ኤርትራ
eritreo	Eritrean	ኤርትራዊ/ት
Etiopia	Ethiopia	ኢትዮጵያ
etiope	Ethiopian	ኢትዮጵያዊ/ት
Europa	Europe	ኤውሮጳ
europeo	European	ኤውሮጳዊ/ት
francese	French	ፈረንሳዊ/ት
Francia	France	ፈረንሳ
Galles	Wales	ዌልስ
gallese	Welsh	ዌልሳዊ/ት
Germania	Germany	ጀርመን
Gran Bretagna	Great Britain	ዓባይ ብሪጣንያ
Grecia	Greece	ግሪኽ
greco	Greek	ግሪኻዊ/ት
Irlanda	Ireland	ኣየርላንድ
irlandese	Irish	ኣየርላንዳዊ/ት
Italia	Italy	ኢጣልያ
italiano	Italian	ኢጣልያዊ/ት
lussemburghese	Luxemburger	ሉክሰምበራዊ/ት
Lussemburgo	Luxemburg	ሉክሰምበርግ

Olanda	Holland	ሆላንድ
olandese	Dutch	ሆላንዳዊ/ት
passaporto	passport	ፓስፖርት
Portogallo	Portugal	ፖርቱጋል
portoghese	Portuguese	ፖርቱጋላዊ/ት
Russia	Russia	ራሻ
russo	Russian	ራሽያዊ/ት
Scozia	Scotland	ስኮትላንድ
scozzese	Scottish	ስኮትላንዳዊ/ት
Spagna	Spain	ስጳኛ
spagnolo	Spanish	ስጳኛዊ/ት
straniero	foreigner	ወጻእተኛ
tedesco	German	ጀርመናዊ/ዊት

Occupations

assistente di volo (m/f)	steward, stewardess	ኣሳሳዪ/ኣሳሳዪት
autista (m/f)	driver	ዘዋራይ/ኣውቲስታ
avvocato	lawyer	ጠበቓ
cameriere (m)	waiter	ኣሳሳዪ
casalinga	housewife	በዓልቲ ሓዳር
commerciante (m/f)	trader	ሸቃጣይ
commercio	trade	ሸቐጥ
commesso	shop-assistant	ሓጋዚ በዓል ድኳን
dentista (m/f)	dentist	ሓኪም ስኒ
direttore (m)	manager	ኣካያዲ ስራሕ (ማናጀር)፡ ዳይረክተር
disoccupato	unemployed	ስራሕ ዘይብሉ፡ ስራሕ ኣልቦ
ditta	firm, company	ትካል፡ ካምፓኒ
dottore (m)	doctor	ሓኪም
essere	to be	ምዃን
fabbrica	factory	ፋብሪካ
farmacista (m/f)	chemist, pharmacist	ኬሚስት፡ ፋርማሲስት
fattoria	farm	ማሕረስ
guadagnare	to earn	ደሞዝ ምርካብ
impiegato	employee	ሰራሕተኛ
infermiere (m)	male nurse	ነርስ
infermiera	nurse	ነርስ
insegnante (m/f)	teacher	መምህር
interessante	interesting	ዘገድስ
lavorare	to work	ምስራሕ

lavoro	job, work	ስራሕ: ዕዮ
macellaio	butcher	በዓል ስጋ፡ ሽያጥስጋ
maestro	teacher (primary)	መምህር
magazzino	store, warehouse	መኽዘን
meccanico	mechanic	ሜካኒክ፡ ዓራይመኪና
medico	doctor	ሓኪም
negozio	shop	ድኳን
operaio	workman	ሰራሕተኛ
padrone (m)	owner	ወናኒ
paga	pay, salary	ደሞዝ
parrucchiere (m)	hairdresser	መሻጢት/መሻጢ
pizzeria	'pizzeria'	ፒሰርያ
poliziotto	policeman	ፖሊስ
posizione (f)	position	ቦታ
professione (f)	profession	ስራሕ፡ ሞያ
professore (m)	teacher, professor	መምህር፡ ፕሮፌሰር
proprietario	owner	ወናኒ/ወናኒት
salario	wage	ደሞዝ
segretario	secretary	ጸሓፊ/ት
stipendio	salary	ደሞዝ
studente (m)	student	ተመሃራይ/ተመሃሪት
tassista (m/f)	taxi-driver	በዓል ታክሲ
trovare un impiego	to find a job	ስራሕ ምርካብ
ufficio	office	ኦፊስ፡ ቤት ጽሕፈት

General descriptions

bambino	child	ቆልዓ
donna	woman	ሰበይቲ
femmina	female	ኣንስተይቲ
figlio	son	ወዲ
maschio	male	ተባዕታይ
ragazza	girl	ጓል
ragazzo	boy	ወዲ
signorina	young lady	ወይዘሪት
uomo	man	ሰብኣይ
celibe (m)	single	ንበይኑ/ንበይና
congratularsi con	to congratulate	እንቋዕ ደስ በለካ ምባል
coniugato	married	ምርዑው
divorziato	divorced	ፍቱሕ
fidanzarsi	to become engaged	ምሕጻይ

Physical Appearance

a mio parere	in my opinion	ብናተይ ርእይቶ
alto	tall	ነዊሕ
anziano	old, elderly	ዓቢ
azzurro	light blue	ሃሳስ ሰማያዊ
baffi (m, pl.)	moustache	ጭሕሚ
barba	beard	ጭሕሚ
basso	short	ሓጺር
bellezza	beauty	ጽባቐ
bello	beautiful, handsome	ጽቡቕ
bianco	white	ጻዕዳ
biondo	fair, blonde	ብጫ
bocca	mouth	ኣፍ
brutto	ugly	ክፉእ
capelli (m, pl.)	hair	ጸጉሪ
carino	pretty	ምጩው
carnagione (f)	complexion	ሕብሪ ቈርበት
castano	brown, hazel	ቡናዊ
chiaro	fair	ብሩህ
corto	short	ሓጺር
denti	teeth	ስኒ
elegante	elegant; smart	ፈሲሕ፡ ኤለጋንተ
giovane	young	መንእሰይ
grasso	fat	ህጡር፡ ስቡሕ
grazioso	pretty	ግሩም
grosso	big	ገዚፍ
lisci (capelli ...)	straight hair	ለማሽ
lungo	long	ነዊሕ
magro	thin	ቀጢን
naso	nose	ኣፍንጫ
nero	black, dark	ጸሊም፡ ጸልማት
occhi	eyes	ኣዒንቲ
occhiali	glasses, spectacles	መነጽር፡ ኦኪያለ
ondulato	wavy	ርሺ ርሺ
orecchino	earring	ኵትሻ
orecchio	ear	እዝኒ
ricci (capelli ...)	curly hair	ጥቕልል ዝበለ ጸጕሪ
robusto	strong, robust	ሓያል፡ ተሪር፡ ድልዱል
snello	slim	ሸጥ ዝበለ፡ ምልምል
somiglianza	likeness	ተመሳሳልነት

sorriso	smile	ፍሽኽታ
statura media	medium height	ማእከላይ ንውሒ
vecchio	old	ኣረጊት
verde	green	ቀጠልያ

Character

abbastanza	rather, enough	እኹል፡ ብሓቂ ወይ ብመጠኑ
allegro	cheerful, merry	ሕጉስ
antipatico	unpleasant	ደስ ዘይብል፡ ዘይሰማማዕ
beneducato	well mannered	ጽቡቕ ጠባይ ዘለዎ ወይ ዘለዋ
bravo	good, clever	ንፉዕ
buffo	funny	መስሓቕ
calmo	calm	ህዱእ
comprensivo	understanding	ዝርዳእ
contento	happy, pleased	ሕጉስ
cortese	polite	ትሑት
divertente	amusing	መስሓቕ፡ ተጻዋታይ
felice	happy	ሕጉስ
geloso	jealous	ቀናእ
gentile	kind	ብሩኽ፡ ሕያዋይ
intelligente	intelligent	በሊሕ
maleducato	bad-mannered	ሕማቕ፡ ጠባይ ዘለዎ
meraviglioso	wonderful	ግሩም፡ ዘደንቕ
molto	much, very	ብዙሕ፡ ኣዝዩ
nervoso	irritable, nervous	ዘሕርቕ፡ ሰንባዲ
noioso	boring	ዘህክይ፡ ዘየገድስ
onesto	honest	እሙን
orgoglioso	proud	ዕቡይ
pazzo	crazy	ጽሉል
pigro	lazy	ህኩይ
piuttosto	rather	ዳርጋ
serio	serious	ረዚን፡ ዘተሓሳስብ
severo	severe, strict	ጽኑዕ፡ ተሪር
simpatico	nice	ተፈታዊ፡ ጽቡቕ
studioso	studious	ተመራማሪ
superbo	proud, haughty	ክሩዕ፡ ዕቡይ
timido	shy, timid	ሓፋር፡ ብሕፍረት ዝፈርህ
triste	sad	ዝሓዘነ፡ ዘሕዝን
vivace	lively	ውዑይ (ንቑሕ) ሰብ

FAMILY

amico	friend	ዓርኪ
babbo	dad	ኣቦ
bambino	child	ቆልዓ
cognato	brother-in-law	ዘማ
cugino	cousin	ወዲ ሓትነ፣ ወዲ ኣኮ ወዲ ሓወቦ፣ ወዲ ኣሞ
famiglia	family	ስድራቤት
figlio	son	ወዲ
figlio unico	only son	እንኮ ወዲ
fratello	brother	ሓው
gemelli	twins	ማናቱ
genitore (m)	parent	ወላዲ፣ ወላዲት
giovane	young	መንእሰይ (ንእሽተይ)
grande	big, grown-up	ዓቢ፣ ዝዓበየ
madre (f)	mother	ኣደ
maggiore	older	ዝዓበየ
mamma	mummy	ማማ፣ ኣደይ
marito	husband	በዓልቤት፣ ሰብኣይ
matrimonio	marriage, wedding	መርዓ
minore	younger	ዝነኣሰ
moglie (f)	wife	በዓልቲቤት፣ ሰበይቲ
nipote (m/f)	nephew, niece, grand-son, grand-daughter	ጓል/ወዲ ኣሞ ጓል/ወዲ ኣኮ፣ ወዲ ወዲ፣ ጓል ጓል
nonno	grand-father	ኣቦሓጎ
nozze (f, pl.)	wedding	መርዓ
numeroso	numerous; large	ብዙሕ፣ ገዚፍ
padre (m)	father	ኣቦ
papà	daddy	ኣቦ፣ ባባ
parente (m/f)	relative	ስድራቤት/ዘመድ
piccolo	small	ንእሽተይ
rassomigliare a	to look like	ምምሳል ን
sorella	sister	ሓውቲ
suocero	father-in-law	ሓሞ
unire	to unite	ምትሕብባር
zio	uncle	ሓወቦ፣ ኣኮ

HOUSE AND HOME

Accommodation and Services

accendere	to switch on	ምውላዕ
acqua	water	ማይ
(al piano) di sopra	upstairs	ላዕለዋይ ደርቢ
(al piano) di sotto	downstairs	ታሕተዋይ ደርቢ
al piano superiore	on the upper floor	ኣብ ላዕለዋይ ደርቢ
al pianterreno	on the ground floor	ኣብ ታሕተዋይ ደርቢ
al primo piano	on the first floor	ኣብ ቀዳማይ ደርቢ
aprire	to open	ምኽፋት
automobile (f)	car	መኪና
balcone (m)	balcony	ሰገነት
bottone/pulsante (m)	button	መልጎም
caldo	hot	ምዉቕ
camera (da letto)	bedroom	መደቀሲ ክፍሊ ቤት
cantina	cellar	ትሕተ ቤታዊ መኽዘን
chiudere	to shut	ምዕጻው
confortevole	comfortable	ምቹእ፡ ጥዑም
cucina	kitchen	ውሻጠ: እንዳ ጸብሒ
dormire	to sleep	ምድቃስ
elettricità	electricity	ሓይሊ ኤለክትሪክ
elettrico	electric	ኤለክትሪክ
entrata	entrance	መእተዊ
fiammifero	match	ክርቢት
finestra	window	መስኮት
fornello	cooker	መስርሒ ጸብሒ
freddo	cold	ቆራሪ
gabinetto	toilet	ዓይኒ ምድሪ፡ ሽቓቕ
garage (m)	garage	ጋራጅ፡ ስፍራ መኪና
ingresso	entrance, hallway	መእተዊ፡ መእተዊ ኣደራሽ
lavandino	wash basin, sink	ላቫንዲኖ፡ መሕጸቢ ገጽ፡ መሕጸቢ ኣቕሑት
macchina	car, machine	መኪና
non funziona	out of order	ካብ ስራሕ ወጻኢ
porta	door	ማዕጾ
premere	to press	ምጽቃጥ፡ ምጥዋቕ
riscaldamento centr.	central heating	መውዓዪ
rubinetto	tap	ቡምባ
sala da pranzo	dining room	መብልዒ ቤት
salotto	sitting-room	መቐበል ኣጋይሽ

scale (f, pl.)	stairs	መደያይቦ፡ ኣስካላ
soggiorno	living-room	ሳሎን፡ መቐበሊ ኣጋይሽ
spegnere	to switch off	ምጥፋእ
stanza	room	ክፍሊ ቤት
(stanza da) bagno	bathroom	ዓይኒ ምድሪ
studio	study	ቤት መጽናዕቲ

Furniture, household equipment and appliances

apparecchiare	to lay the table	ጣውላ ምቕራብ
armadio	wardrobe	መስቀል ክዳውንቲ
arredare	to furnish	ምቕራብ ኣቕሑ ናይ ገዛ
asciugamano	hand towel	ናይ ኢድ ሽጎማኖ፡ ናይ ኢድ መሐበሲ
aspirapolvere (m)	vacuum-cleaner	ኰስታሪት መኪና
bagno (vasca da ...)	bath	መሕጸቢ
bicchiere (m)	glass	ብርጭቆ
bottiglia	bottle	ጥርሙዝ
caffettiera	coffee pot	ጀበና
casseruola	saucepan	ድስቲ
cassetto	drawer	ተመዛዚ
coltello	knife	ካራ
congelatore (m)	freezer	መዝሓሊ
coperta	cover, blanket	መሸፈኒ፡ ኮቦርታ
cosa	thing	ነገር
credenza	sideboard	ኮሞዲኖ
cucchiaino	teaspoon	ናይ ሻሂ ማንካ፡ ናይ ቡን ማንካ
cucchiaio	spoon	ማንካ
cucina	kitchen	ውሻጠ፡ እንዳጸብሒ
cuscino	cushion, pillow	መተርኣስ
dentifricio	toothpaste	ኮልጌት
disco	record	ዲስክ
divano	settee	ሩቦ፡ ሶፋ
doccia	shower	ሻወር
elettricità	electricity	ሓይሊ ኤለክትሪክ
elettrico	electric	ኤለክትሪክ
elettrodomestici	electric household appliances	ናይ ገዛ ኤለክትሪክ መተዓየዪ
federa	pillow-case	ሽፋን መተርኣስ
forchetta	fork	ፎርኬታ

forno	oven	እቶን
frigorifero	refrigerator	መዝሓሊ፡ ፍሪጅ
lampada	lamp	ፋኑስ፡ ፋና
lampadina	light bulb	ላምፓዲና
lavastoviglie (f)	dish-washer	መሕጸቢ ድስቲ፡ ቢያቲ ... ወዘተ
lavatrice (f)	washing machine	መሕጸቢት ክዳን
lenzuolo	sheet	ኣንሶላ
letto	bed	ዓራት
libreria	bookcase	መትሓዚ መጽሓፍ
lucidatrice (f)	floor-polisher	ቼራ
mobile (m)	piece of furniture	ኣቕሓ
orologio	clock	ሰዓት
padella	pan	ባዴላ
parecchi	many, several	ሓያሎ፡ ብዙሕ
pattumiera	dustbin	እንዳ ጕሓፍ
pentola	pot; pan	ባዴላ
pianoforte (m)	piano	ፒያኖ
piattino	saucer	ንእሽቶ ቢያቲ
piatto	plate, dish	ቢያቲ
poltrona	arm-chair	ሶፋ
portacenere (m)	ash-tray	መንገፍ ሽጋራ
quadro	picture	ስእሊ
radio (f)	radio	ራድዮ
registratore (m)	tape-recorder	ቴፕ
sapone (m)	soap	ሳምና
scaffale (m)	shelf	ስካፋለ
sedia	chair	መንበር
sparecchiare	to clear the table	ጣውላ ምጽራይ
spazzolino da denti	toothbrush	ብራሽ ስኒ
sveglia	alarm clock	መበራበሪት ሰዓት
tappeto	carpet	ምንጻፍ
tazza	cup	ጣሳ
tazzina	coffee-cup	ፍንጃል
tegame	saucepan	መቕለዊ፡ ባዴላ፡ ድስቲ
teiera	tea-pot	በራድ
televisione (f)	television	ተለቪዥን
tende	curtains	መጋረጃ
tovaglia	table cloth	ክዳን ጣውላ
tovagliolo	napkin, serviette	መድረዝ ኣፍ
video registratore	video recorder	ቀዳሒት ቪደዮ

GEOGRAPHICAL SURROUNDINGS AND WEATHER

Location

abitante (m)	inhabitant	ተቐማጢ
c'è, ci sono	there is, there are	ኣሎ/ኣለዉ
camminare	to walk	ምኻድ
campagna (in ...)	country (in the ...)	ገጠር (ኣብ ...)
capitale (f)	capital	ርእሰ ከተማ
centro	centre	ማእከል
chilometro	kilometre	ኪሎመትር
cielo	sky	ሰማይ
città (in ...)	city, town (in the ...)	ከተማ (ኣብ ...)
dove, dov'è	where, where is	ኣበይ፣ ኣበይ ኢዩ
est (m)	east	ምብራቕ
giro	tour	ዙረት
gita	excursion, trip	ዑደት/መገሻ
località	locality, place	ቦታ
lontano da	far from	ርሑቕ ካብ
mare; (al ...)	sea; (at the seaside)	ባሕሪ (ኣብ ገምገም)
mondo	world	ዓለም
montagna (in ...)	mountain (in the ...s)	እምባ (ኣብ እምባታት)
nord (m)	north	ሰሜን
ovest (m)	west	ምዕራብ
passeggiare	to stroll, to walk	ምዝዋር
passeggiata	stroll, walk	ዙረት
periferia (in ...)	suburb (in the ...)	ከባቢ (ኣብ ...)
regione (f)	region	ሃገር/ኣውራጃ
sud (m)	south	ደቡብ
vedere	to see	ምርኣይ
visitare	to visit	ምብጻሕ
vista	view	ምርኢት

Amenities/features of interest

aeroporto	airport	መዓርፎ ነፈርቲ
albergo	hotel	መዕረፍ ኣጋይሽ፣ ሆተል
altro	other	ካልእ
antico	ancient	ጥንቲ
architettura	architecture	ስነ-ህንጻ
abbazia	abbey	ኣቕሽሽቲ ዝነብሩሉ ርሻን
bello	beautiful	ጽቡቕ

bosco	wood	ጫካ
brutto	ugly	ክፉእ
campeggio	camping site	መዕረፊ ቦታ
carta geografica	map	ኣትላስ
castello	castle	ርሻን (ናይ ነገስታት ... ወዘተ)
cattedrale (f)	cathedral	ዓቢ ቤተክርስትያን
chiesa	church	ቤተ ክርስትያን
cinema (m)	cinema	ሲነማ
collina	hill	ኩርባ
discoteca	discotheque	ዲስኮተክ
duomo	cathedral	ዓቢ ቤተክርስትያን
edificio	building	ህንጻ
epoca	age, epoch	ዘመን
fabbrica	factory	ፋብሪካ
fattoria	farm	ሕርሻ
fiume (m)	river	ውሕጅ
fontana	fountain	ዓይኒ ማይ
foresta	forest	ዱር
interessante	interesting	ኣድላዪ፡ ኣገዳሲ
isola	island	ደሴት
lago	lake	ቀላይ
moderno	modern	ዘመናዊ
monumento	monument	ሓወልቲ (መዘከር)
municipio	town-hall	ምምሕድዳር ከተማ (ቦታ)
museo	museum	ቤተመዘክር
paesaggio	landscape, scenery	መልክዕ ምድሪ (ኣቀማምጣ መሬት)
panorama (m)	view, panorama	ግሩም ምርኢት በረኻ
parco	park	ናይ ኣታኽልቲ ስፍራ፡ ጠጠው መበሊ ቦታ
piscina	swimming pool	መሐምበሲ ቦታ
ponte (m)	bridge	ድልድል
settentrionale	northern	ሰሜናዊ ሸነኽ
spiaggia	beach	ገምገም ባሕሪ
stadio	stadium	ስታድዮም (ናይ ኩዕሶ እግሪ መጻወቲ ሜዳ)
stazione (f)	station	ጣብያ (ነቑጣ)
storico	historic	ታሪኻዊ
teatro	theatre	ትያትር
villaggio	village	ዓዲ

Weather

asciutto	dry	ደረቕ
atmosfera	atmosphere	ከባቢ ኣየር
autunno	autumn	ቀውዒ
brezza	breeze	ንፉስ (ዝሑል)
caldo	hot	ሙቐት
che tempo fa?	what's the weather like?	ናይ ኣየር ኩነታት እንታይ ይመስል፧
cielo	sky	ሰማይ
clima (m)	climate	ናይ ኣየር ኩነታት
coperto	cloudy, overcast	ደመና
estate (f)	summer	ክረምቲ
far bel tempo/bello	to be good weather	ጽቡቕ ኩነታት ኣየር
brutto tempo	to be bad weather	ሕማቕ ኩነታት ኣየር
caldo	to be hot	ሃሩር ኣሎ
freddo	to be cold	ቍሪ ኣሎ
fulmine (m)	lightning	በርቂ
ghiaccio	ice	በረድ
grandine (f)	hail	በረድ ዘለዎ ማይ
inverno	winter	ክረምቲ
lampo	flash of lightning	በርቂ
mite	mild	ደሓን
nebbia	fog	ግመ
neve (f)	snow	በረድ
nevicare	to snow	በረድ ምውዳቕ
nuvola	cloud	ደመና
pioggia	rain	ዝናም
piovere	to rain	ምዝናም
piovigginare	to drizzle	ምኽፋይ
primavera	spring	ቀውዒ
secco	dry	ንቑጽ
sereno	clear, cloudless	ብሩህ፡ ደመና ዘይብሉ
sole (m)	sun	ጸሓይ
soleggiato	sunny	ጸሓያዊ
stagione (f)	season	ክፍሊ ዓመት፡ ወርሓት፡ እዋናት
temperatura	temperature	ዓቐን ምቔት
tempesta	storm	ሕማቕ ኩነታት ኣየር
temporale (m)	thunder storm	ነጐዳ ዝተሓወሶ ኣውሎ ንፉስ (ማዕበል)
umidità	humidity	ጠሊ
vento	wind	ንፉስ

TRAVEL AND TRANSPORT

Public Transport

bagaglio	luggage	ሳንጣ፡ ባልጃ
biglietteria	ticket office	ቲኬት መሸጢ ቤት
biglietto	ticket	ቲኬት
binario	platform	መድረኽ
conducente (m/f)	driver	ዘዋራይ
controllore (m)	inspector	ተቖጻጻሪ፡ መርማሪ
corriera	coach	ኣውቶቡስ
cuccetta	couchette	መደቀሲ (ኣብ ባቡር ምድሪ)
fermata	stop	ጠጠው መበሊ
ferrovia	railway	መገዲ ባቡር
finestrino	window	መስኮት
nave (f)	ship	መርከብ
orario	timetable	ግዜ፡ ሰዓት
partire	to leave	ምኻድ
passeggero	passenger	ገያሻይ/መንገደኛ
prenotare	to book	ምምዝጋብ
pullman (m)	coach	ኣሰልጣኒ
sala d'aspetto	waiting room	መጸበዩ ክፍሊ
stazione (f)	station	ፈሮቪያ
tassì	taxi	ታክሲ
treno	train	ባቡር
ufficio informazioni	information office	ናይ ሓበሬታ ቤ/ጽሕፈት
valigia	suitcase	ሳንጣ፡ ባልጃ
viaggiatore (m)	traveller	ገያሻይ

Travel by Air/Sea

aereo	aeroplane	ነፋሪት
assistente di volo (m/f)	steward, stewardess	ናይ ነፋሪት ኣሳሳዪት
atterrare	to land	ምብጻሕ፡ ምውራድ
carta d'imbarco	boarding pass	መስቀሊ ፈቓድ
cintura di sicurezza	safety belt	መቐነቲ
controllo	check	ቊጽጽር
crociera	cruise	መገሻ
decollare	to take off	ምትንሳእ
dogana	customs	ዱጋና
frontiera	frontier	ዶብ

'hostess'	air hostess	ሆስተስ
hovercraft (m)	hovercraft	ሆቨርክራፍት
imbarcare	to embark, board	ምድያብ
nave (f)	ship	መርከብ
passaporto	passport	ፓስፖርት
pilota	pilot	ፓይሎት፥ ዘዋሪ ነፋሪት
porto	port, harbour	ወደብ፥ ማርሳ
sbarcare	to disembark	ምውራድ
traghetto (nave ...)	ferry (boat)	መሰጋገሪት መርከብ
traversata	crossing	መተሓላለፊ
uscita	exit, gate	መውጽኢ
volare	to fly	ምንፋር
volo	flight	በረራ

Private Transport

agente di polizia	policeman	ፖሊስ
assicurazione	insurance	መድሕን
autista (m/f)	driver	ዘዋሪ መኪና
autostrada	motorway	መገዲ መኪና
batteria	battery	ባተሪ
benzina	petrol	ነዳዲ
bicicletta	bicycle	ብሽክለታ
cambio	gear stick	ማርሻ
camion (m)	lorry	ናይ ጽዕነት መኪና
candela	spark plug	ካንዴላ
casco	helmet	ሄልመት፥ ወትሃደራዊ ቆብዕ
cintura di sicurezza	seat belt	መዕጠቒ
copertone (m)	tyre	ጎማ (ናይ መኪና ...)
dare la precedenza	to give way	መገዲ ምሃብ
distributore (di ben.)	petrol pump	ናይ ነዳዲ መዐደሊ
forare	to have a puncture	ጎማ ነኽሉ
frenare	to brake	ፍሬኖ ምሓዝ
freno	brake	ፍሬኖ
frizione	clutch	ፍረስዮን
furgone (m)	van	መኪና ጽዕነት
gomma	tyre	ጎማ (ናይ መኪና ...)
gonfiare	to inflate	ምንፋሕ
guidare	to drive	ምዝዋር
incidente (m)	accident	ሓደጋ

incrocio	crossroads	ተሓላለፍቲ መገድታት
ingorgo	traffic jam	ናይ ትራፊክ ጸዕቂ
lavaggio	washing; car wash	ምሕጻብ፡ መኪና ምሕጻብ
lavori in corso	work in progress	ኣብ መስርሕ ዘሎ ዕዮ
limite di velocità	speed limit	ናይ ፍጥነት እገዳ
macchina	car	መኪና
moto (cicletta) (f)	motorcycle	ቱግቱግ፡ ሞቶ
motore (m)	engine	ሞተር
multa	fine	መቕጻዕቲ
nafta	diesel	ናፍታ
noleggiare	to hire	ምክራይ
olio	oil	ዘይቲ
ore di punta	rush hours	ናይ ጉያ ጉያ ሰዓታት
panne (in ...)	breakdown	መስበርቲ
parcheggiare	to park	ምዕሻግ
patente (f)	driving licence	መዘወሪ ፍቓድ
pezzi di ricambio	spare parts	መለዋወጢ
pieno; (fare il ...)	full; (to fill it up)	ምሉእ
pneumatico	tyre	ጎማ
pompa (di benzina)	petrol pump	ፖምፓ
posteggio	parking space	መጸግዒ
pressione (f)	pressure	ጸቕጢ
rallentare	to slow down	ቀስ ምባል
ruota	wheel	ጎማ፡ ቸርክዮ
scontro	bump, collision	ጎንጺ
semaforo	traffic lights	ሰማፎሮ
senso (a ... unico)	one way	ብሓደ ሸነኽ ዝኸይድ
senza piombo (benzina)	unleaded (petrol)	ፒዮምቦ ዘይብሉ
sorpassare	to overtake	ምሕላፍ
sosta	parking	ፓርኪን፡ መዓሸጊ
targa	number plate	ታርጋ
traffico	traffic	ትራፊክ
velocità	speed	ፍጥነት
volante (m)	steering wheel	ስተርሶ፡ መዘወሪ

HOLIDAYS

abbronzarsi	to get a tan	ጸሓይ ምውቃዕ
abbronzato	sun-tanned	ጸሓይ ዝተወቕዐ
affittare	to rent, to hire	ምክራይ
agenzia di viaggi	travel agency	ቤት ጽሕፈት ወኪል ጉዕዞ
bagnino	lifeguard	ሓላዊ
barca	boat	ጀልባ
benvenuto	welcome	መርሓባ
costume da bagno	bathing costume	መሐንበሲ ክዳን
crema solare	suntan lotion	ሳንታን ሎሽን
diapositiva	slide, transparency	ስላይድ
estero (all'...)	abroad	ወጻኢ ሃገር
ferie	holidays	በዓላት
foto (f)	photograph	ስእሊ
giro	trip	መገሻ
gita	excursion; school trip	መዘናግዒ,መገሻ
guida	guide	ሓባሪ
in macchina	by car	ብመኪና
lago	lake	ቀላይ
macchina fotografica	camera	ካሜራ፡ መስኣሊት
mare (m)	sea	ባሕሪ
montagna	mountain	ጎቦ
monumento	monument	ሓወልቲ፡ መዘከር
occhiali da sole	sun-glasses	መረጼን ጸሓይ
ombrellone (m)	beach umbrella	ናይ ገምገም ባሕሪ ጽላል
ospitalità	hospitality	ጽቡቕ ኣቀባብላ ጋሻ
rullino/rollino	film (for camera)	ፊልም (ንካሜራ)
sabbia	sand	ሑጻ
sciare	to ski	ምንሽርታት (ኣብ በረድ)
sedia a sdraio	deck-chair	ኮፍ መበሊ
sole (m)	sun	ጸሓይ
spiaggia	beach	ገምገም ባሕሪ
turismo	tourism	ቱሪዝም
turista (m/f)	tourist	ቱሪስት
vacanza	holiday	በዓል
visitare	to visit	ምብጻሕ

TOURIST INFORMATION

(see also Hotel and Free Time)

albergo	hotel	ሆቴል
cartina geografica	(small) map	ንእሽቶይ ማፕ (መሐበሪት)
cercare	to look for	ምድላይ
cinema (m)	cinema	ሲነማ
città	town, city	ከተማ
concerto	concert	ኮንሰርት
dépliant (m)	leaflet, brochure	ቆጽሊ፡ ሓጺር ናይ ጽሑፍ መግለጺ
divertimenti	amusements	ዘስሕቕ፡ ዘሕጉስ፡ ዘደስት
giocare (a tennis ...)	to play (tennis...)	ምጽዋት (ተኒስ ...)
informare	to inform	ምሕባር ምሕታት
museo	museum	ቤተ መዘክር
musica	music	ሙዚቃ
negozio	shop	ድኳን
opera	opera	ኦፔራ
opuscolo	booklet,brochure	ሓጺር ናይ ጽሑፍ መግለጺ
parco	park	ኣትክልቲ ዘለዎ፡ መዘናግዒ ቦታ
pianta (della città)	map (of the town)	ማፕ፡ መሓበሪ (ናይ ከተማ)
regione (f)	region, area	ዞባ፡ ቦታ
ristorante (m)	restaurant	ቤት መግቢ
spettacolo	show, performance	ምርኢት
sport (m)	sport	ስፖርት
teatro	theatre	ትያትር
ufficio informazioni	information office	ናይ ሓበሬታ ቤ/ጽሕፈት

HOTEL

albergo	hotel	ኣልበርጎ
ascensore (m)	lift	ሊፍት
bagagli (m, pl.)	luggage	ሳንጣ
camera	room	ክፍሊ ቤት
... per due persone	double ...	ድርብ
... per una persona	single ...	ንጽል
... matrimoniale	double ...	ድርብ
... a due letti	... with twin beds	ምስ ክልተ ዓራት
... a un letto	... with a single bed	ምስ ሓንቲ ዓራት
... con (il) bagno	... with a bath	ምስ መሕጸቢ ክፍሊ
... con (la) doccia	... with a shower	ምስ ሻወር
chiave (f)	key	መፍትሕ
completo	full	ምሉእ
compreso, incluso	inclusive	ዘጠቓልል
conto	bill, amount	ሕሳብ፡ ብዝሒ፡ መጠን ገንዘብ
direttore (m)	manager	ኣካያዲ ስራሕ፡ ዳይረክተር
direzione (la ...)	management	ምምሕዳር
padrone (m)	owner	ወናኒ
pagare	to pay	ምኽፋል
passaporto	passport	ፓስፖርት
piano	floor, storey	ደርቢ
pianterreno	ground floor	ታሕተዋይ ደርቢ
portare	to carry, to bring, to take	ምስካም፡ ምምጻእ፡ ምውሳድ
prenotare	to book	ምምዝጋብ፡ ክፍሊ ምሓዝ
ricevuta	receipt	ሪቸቡታ፡ ቅብሊት
riservare	to reserve	ኣቐዲምካ ምሓዝ
ristorante (m)	restaurant	ቤት መግቢ
scale	stairs	መደያይቦ፡ ኣስካላ
telefono	telephone	ተለፎን
televisore (m)	television set	ተለቪዥን
uscita di sicurezza	emergency exit	ናይ ሓደጋ መውጽኢ ቦታ
valigia	suitcase	ሳንጣ ወይ ባልጃ
vista	view	ርእይቶ
visto	visa	ፍቓድ (መውጽኢ ወይ መእተዊ)

FOOD AND DRINK

General

aceto	vinegar	አቸቶ
acqua minerale	mineral water	ማይ ጋዝ
aranciata	orangeade	ኣራንቻታ
arrosto	roast	ዝተቐልወ ዝተጠብሰ
bere	to drink	ምስታይ
bevanda	drink	መስተ
birra	beer	ቢራ
biscotto	biscuit	ብሽኮቲ
brindare	to toast	ንጥዕና ምባል
buon appetito	enjoy your meal	ጽቡቕ ሸውሃት ይግበረልካ
burro	butter	ጠስሚ፡ ቡሮ
caffellatte (m)	white coffee	ጸባን ቡንን
caffettiera	coffee pot/maker	ጀበና
caffè (m)	coffee	ቡን
caldo	hot	ውዑይ
cappuccino	cappuccino	ካፑቺኖ (ጸባን ቡንን)
caramelle	sweets	ምቁር ነገራት
cena	dinner; supper	ድራር
cibo	food	መግቢ
cincin!	cheers!	ንጥዕና
cioccolata	chocolate	ችኮላታ
colazione (prima ...)	breakfast	ቍርሲ
dolce, dessert (m)	sweet, dessert	ዶልቺ፡ ፍረታት
formaggio	cheese	ፉርማጆ
frittata	omelet	እተቐልወ እንቛቝሖ
gelato	ice cream	ጀላቶ
lasagne (f, pl.)	lasagna	ላዛኛ (ፓስታ)
latte (m)	milk	ጸባ
limonata	lemonade	ጽማቝ ለሚን
macedonia	fruit salad	ማቸዶንያ
minestra	soup	ናይ ኣሕምልቲ መረቕ
mozzarella	'mozzarella'	ሞዛሬላ
olio di semi	vegetable oil	ናይ ኣሕምልቲ ዘይቲ
pane (m)	bread	ሕብስቲ፡ ባኒ
patate fritte	chips, French fries	ምትርታር ቅልዋ ድንሽ
patatine	crisps, chips	ዝተጠብሰ ድንሽ
piccante	spicy, hot	ቀመማዊ፡ መሪር

pizza	pizza	ፒሳ
ravioli	ravioli	ራቭዮሊ
ricetta	recipe	መምርሒ ኣሰራርሓ መግቢ
riso	rice	ሩዝ
sale (m)	salt	ጨው
salute (alla ...!)	cheers!	ንጥዕና
spremuta	fresh fruit juice	ሓድሽ ናይ ፍሩታ ጽማቕ
succo di frutta	fruit juice	ናይ ፍሩታ ጽማቕ
tè (m)	tea	ሻሂ
torta	cake	ፓስተ
uovo	egg	እንቋቝሖ
vino (bianco, rosso)	wine (white, red)	ቪኖ (ጻዕዳ፡ ቀይሕ/ሮዛ)
zucchero	sugar	ሽኮር

Café, Restaurant and other Public Places

acqua	water	ማይ
bar (m)	bar, café	ባር
bicchiere (m)	glass	ብርጭቆ
birra	beer	ቢራ
caffè (m)	coffee (... house)	ቡን፡ ቡና ቤት፡ ካፌ፡ ባር
cameriere (m)	waiter	ኣሰላፊ
conto	bill	ናይ መኽፈሊ ቅጺ
contorno	vegetables, side dish	ኣሕምልቲ መወሰኽታ
espresso	espresso (coffee)	ቡን (ቅልጡፍ ቡን)
fiasco	flask	ፊያስኮ
ghiaccio	ice	በረድ
litro	litre	ሊትሮ
panino; (... imbottito)	roll (filled roll, sandwich)	ጥቕላል (ዝተመልአ ጥቕላል ሳንድዊች)
piatto (del giorno)	dish (of the day)	ናይዚ መዓልቲ መግቢ
pizzeria	'pizzeria'	ፒሰርያ (ፒሳ ዝሸየጠሉ ቤት መግቢ)
primo (piatto)	first (course)	መጀመርያ (ቀዳማይ) መግቢ
ristorante (m)	restaurant	ቤት መግቢ
secondo (piatto)	second (course)	ካልኣይ (ሴኮንዶ)
spumante (m)	'sparkling wine'	ሹሽ ዝብል ቪኖ፡ ዘንጸባርቕ ቪኖ
tovagliolo	napkin	ናይ ጣውላ ምንጻፍ

Fruit and vegetables

aglio	garlic	ሽጉርቲ ጻዕዳ
albicocca	apricot	ሚሽሚሽ (ዓይነት ፍረ)
ananas (m)	pineapple	ኣናናስ
anguria	water melon	ብርጭቕ
arancia	orange	ኣራንሺ
banana	banana	ባናና
carciofo	artichoke	ካርቾፊ፡ ዓይነት ሓምሊ
carota	carrot	ካሮት
cavolfiore (m)	cauliflower	ካውሎ ፍዮሪ
cavolo	cabbage	ካውሎ ካፑቺ
cetriolo	cucumber	ዚኩኒ
ciliegia	cherry	ቸሪ
cipolla	onion	ሽጉርቲ ቀዪሕ
fagioli	beans	ባልደንጓ
fagiolini	French beans	ባልደንጓ ፈረንሳ
fragola	strawberry	ፍራጎላ
frutta	fruit	ፍሩታ
fungo	mushroom	ቃንጥሻ ዓሶ
insalata	salad, lettuce	ሰላጣ
lampone (m)	raspberry	ዓጋም
limone (m)	lemon	ለሚን
mango	mango	ማንጉስ
mela	apple	ቱፋሕ፡ ሜለ
melanzana	aubergine	መለንዛኒ
melone (m)	melon	መሎን
oliva	olive	ኣውሊዕ
papaia	papaw	ፓፓያ
patata	potato	ድንሽ
pepe (m)	pepper	ጉዕ
peperone	pepper (red ...)	ጉዕ (ቀይሕ/ቀጠልያ)
pera	pear	ፐረ
pesca	peach	ኩኸ
piselli	peas	ዓይኒዓተር
pomodoro	tomato	ኮሚደሮ
pompelmo	grapefruit	ናርገ
porro	leek	ሊክ
sedano	celery	ሰደኖ
uva (f, sing.)	grapes	ወይኒ
verdura (f, sing.)	vegetables, greens	ኣቕጽልቲ

Meat and Fish

agnello	lamb	ዕየት
aragosta	lobster	ሎብስተር
baccalà (m)	dried salted cod	ንቑጽ ዓሳ
bistecca, (...ai ferri)	steak, (grilled ...)	ቢስቴካ (ዝተጠብሰ...)
bollito	boiled meat	ዝተጠጠቐ ስጋ
capretto	kid	ማሕስእ
coniglio	rabbit	ማንቲለ
cozze	mussels	ተምሪ ባሕሪ (ዓይነት ኣሮነ)
frittura di pesce	mixed fried fish	ዝተሓዋወሰ ቅልውላው ዓሳ
frutti di mare	seafood	ናይ ባሕሪ መግቢ
gamberetti	shrimps/prawns	ሽሪምፕ
granchio	crab	ክራብ
maiale (m)	pork	ናይ ሓሰማ ስጋ
manzo	beef	ናይ ብዕራይ ስጋ
merluzzo	cod	ኮድ (ዓይነት ዓሳ)
montone (m)	mutton	ናይ በጊዕ ስጋ
mortadella	mortadella	ሞርታዴላ
ostrica	oyster	ኦይስተር
pesce (m)	fish	ዓሳ
pollo	chicken	ደርሆ
prosciutto	ham	ሰለፍ ሓሰማ
salame (m)	salami	ብሽጉርቲ ጻዕዳን ጨውን እተቓመመ ሓሰማ
salmone (m)	salmon	ሳልሞን (ዓይነት ዓሳ)
sardina	sardine	ሰርዲን
scampi	scampi	ስካምፐ
sogliola	sole	ዓሳመሴ
tacchino	turkey	ታኪን
tonno	tuna	ቱና (ዓሳ)
trota	trout	ትሮት
vitello	veal	ስጋ ምራኽ
vongola	clam	ክላም

SHOPPING

Shops

abbigliamento (n. di ...)	clothes shop	ናይ ክዳውንቲ ድኳን
alimentari (negozio di ...)	grocer's (shop)	ድኳን፡ ግሮሰሪ
cartoleria	stationery (shop)	ናይ ጽሕፈት መሳርሒ መሸጢ
edicola	newspaper kiosk	ናይ ጋዜጣ መሸጢ
farmacia	pharmacy; chemist's	ቤት መሸጣ መድሃኒት
fioraio	florist	ቤት ዕምበባ
fruttivendolo	greengrocer's	ሸያጢ ኣሕምልትን ፍሩታታትን
gelateria	ice-cream (shop)	እንዳ ጀላቶ
gioielleria	jeweller's (shop)	እንዳ ወርቅን ካልእ ዕንቍታትን
giornalaio	newsagent	ሸያጢ ጋዜጣ
grande magazzino	department store	መኽዘን
lavanderia	laundry	ቤት ሕጽቦ
libreria	bookshop	ቤት መጻሕፍቲ
macelleria	butcher's (shop)	ቤት መሸጣ ስጋ
mercato	market	ሹቕ
panetteria/fornaio	baker's (shop)	ቤት ሕብስቲ
parrucchiere (m)	hairdresser	መሻጢት
pasticceria	confectioner's (shop)	እንዳ ምቁር ሕብስቲ
pescheria	fishmonger's (shop)	እንዳ ዓሳ
profumeria	perfumer's shop	ቤት ጨና
salumeria	delicatessen (shop)	ግሮሰሪ
supermercato	supermarket	ሱፐርማርከት
tabaccheria	tobacconist's (shop)	እንዳ ሽጋራ

Clothes

calze	socks, stockings	ካልሲ
camicia	shirt	ካምቻ
cappello	hat	ቆብዕ
cappotto	(over) coat	ካፖት
cintura	belt	ቍልፌ
costume da bagno	bathing costume	መሐንበሲ ክዳን
cravatta	tie	ክራባታ
fazzoletto	handkerchief	መንዲል
giacca	jacket	ጃኬት፡ ጁባ
gonna	skirt	ጎና
impermeabile (m)	raincoat	ናይ ማይ ጁባ
maglia	jersey	ማልያ

pantaloni, (paio di)	trousers, (pair of)	ስረ
pigiama (m)	pyjamas	ናይ ለይቲ ክዳን፡ ፒጃማ
scarpa	shoe	ጫማ
stivale (m)	boot	ቡት
vestiti/abiti	clothes	ክዳን
vestito	suit, dress	ክዳውንቲ

Materials

argento	silver	ብሩር
carta	paper	ወረቐት
cotone (m)	cotton	ጡጥ
ferro	iron	ሓጺን
lana	wool	ሱፍ
legno	wood	ዕንጸይቲ
metallo	metal	ሓጺን
nailon	nylon	ናይሎን
oro	gold	ወርቂ
pelle	leather	ቆርበት
plastica	plastic	ፕላስቲክ
seta	silk	ሃሪ፡ ሓሪር
stoffa	cloth, material	ክዳን፡ ኣቕሓ
velluto	velvet	ዓለባ ሃሪ
vetro	glass	ቬትሮ፡ ጥርሙዝ

Colours

arancione	orange	ሕብሪ ኣራንቺ
bianco	white	ጻዕዳ
celeste	light blue	ሃሳስ ሰማያዊ
chiaro	light	ብሩህ
colore	colour	ሕብሪ
giallo	yellow	ብጫ
grigio	grey	ሓሙኽሽታይ
marrone	brown	ቡናዊ
nero	black	ጸሊም
rosa	pink	ሮዛ
rosso	red	ቀይሕ
scuro	dark	ድሙቕ ጸሊም
verde	green	ቀጠልያ
viola	violet	ሊላ

SERVICES

Post Office & Telephone

all'estero	abroad	ወጻኢ
ascoltare	to listen	ምስማዕ
attimo	moment	እዋን
bolletta	bill	ሕሳብ
buca delle lettere	letter box, post box	ናይ ደብዳቤ ሳጹን
busta	envelope	ፖስታ
cabina (telefonica)	telephone box	ናይ ተሌፎን ሳጹን
cartolina (postale)	postcard	ፖስታ ካርድ
centralino	telephone exchange	ማእከል ተለፎን
centralinista (m/f)	operator	ሓባሪ ኦፕሬተር
chi parla?	who is speaking?	መን ክብል፧
destinatario	addressee	ደብዳቤ ዝቕበል ሰብ
elenco telefonico	telephone directory	መሐበሪ-ተለፎን
fare il numero	to dial the number	ተለፎን ምድዋል
francobollo	stamp	ቴምብር
impostare/imbucare	to post	ምልኣኽ
indirizzo	address	ኣድራሻ
interno	extension	ኤክስተንሽን
lettera	letter	ደብዳበ
libero	free	ናጻ
mittente (m/f)	sender	ለኣኺ
numero	number	ቍጽሪ
occupato	engaged	ትሕዝቲ
pacchetto (postale)	(small) parcel	ንእሽቶ ፓኮ
pacco	parcel	ፓኮ
Pagine Gialle	Yellow Pages	ረከላም
posta	mail	ደብዳበታት
postino/portalettere	postman	በዓል ፖስታ
prefisso	area code (telephone)	ናይ ዞን ኮድ
pronto!	hallo!	ሃሎ/ሃለው
richiamare	to call back	ዲጊምካ ምጽዋዕ
segreteria telefonica	answerphone	መላሺ.ት ተሌፎን
spedire	to send	ምስዳድ
suonare	to ring	ምድዋል
telefonare	to telephone	ምድዋል
telefono	telephone	ተሌፎን
ufficio postale	post office	ቤት ጽሕፈት ፖስታ

Bank or Exchange Office

agenzia di cambio	exchange bureau	መቀይየሪ ቤት ጽሕፈት
assegno (bancario)	cheque	ቸክ
banca	bank	ባንክ
banconota	banknote	ናይ ባንክ ወረቐት
Birr	Birr	ብር
cambiare	to change	ምልዋጥ
cambio	exchange	ምልውዋጥ፡ ዋጋ ለውጢ
carta assegni	cheque card	ቸክ ካርድ
carta di credito	credit card	መቐበሊ ገንዘብ
cassa	cash desk, till	ካሳ
commissione (f)	commission	ኮሚስዮን
conto corrente	current account	ተንቀሳቓሲ ሕሳብ
denaro	money	ገንዘብ
firmare	to sign	ምፍራም
interesse (m)	interest	ወለድ
istituto di credito	bank	ባንክ
libretto di assegni	cheque book	ናይ ቸክ መጽሓፍ
Lira	Lira	ሊረ
Nakfa	Nakfa	ናቕፋ
modulo	form	ቅርጺ
moneta	coin	ሰልዲ (ሓጺን)
passaporto	passport	ፓስፖርት
per cento	per cent	ሚእታዊት
prestito	loan	ልቓሕ
ritirare	to withdraw	ገንዘብ ምውጻእ
saldo	balance	ሚዛን
soldi (m, pl.)	money	ገንዘብ
spiccioli (m, pl.)	small change	ውሑድ ማልስ (ሽሩፍ)
Sterlina	Pound (sterling)	ፓውንድ
travellers' cheque	travellers' cheque	ናይ መንገደኛ ቸክ
ufficio di cambio	bureau de change	ቤት ጽሕፈት ሸርፌ ገንዘብ
valore	value	ዋጋ
valuta	currency	ባጤራ

HEALTH

General

aiuto	help	ሓገዝ
aver mal di denti	to have a tooth ache	ስኒ ምሕማም
... gola	... sore throat	ጐረሮ ምሕማም
... schiena	... back ache	ሕቖ ምሕማም
... stomaco	... stomach ache	ከስዐ ምሕማም
... testa	... head ache	ርእሲ ምሕማም
ammalarsi	to fall ill	ምሕማም
ammalato	ill	ሕሙም
bocca	mouth	ኣፍ
braccio	arm	ቅልጽም
caldo	hot, warm	ውዑይ፣ ምዉቕ
caviglia	ankle	ኩርኹሬ
cuore (m)	heart	ልቢ
dito	finger	ኣጻብዕ
fegato	liver	ጸላም ከብዲ
freddo	cold	ዝሑል
gamba	leg	እግሪ
ginocchio	knee	ብርኪ
lingua	tongue	መልሓስ
malato	ill	ምሕማም
mano (f)	hand	ኢድ
occhio	eye	ዓይኒ
orecchio	ear	እዝኒ
osso	bone	ዓጽሚ
pelle (f)	skin	ቆርበት
pericoloso	dangerous	ሓደገኛ
piede (m)	foot	እግሪ
salute (f)	health	ጥዕና
sangue (m)	blood	ደም
spalla	shoulder	መንኩብ
stare meglio	to feel/be better	ምምሕያሽ
va bene	it is all right, fine	ደሓን ኢዩ

Illness and injury

annegare	to drown	ምጥሓል
aspirina	aspirin	ኣስፕሪን
attacco	fit, stroke, attack	ዘለምስ ሕማም፡ መጥቃዕቲ
benda	bandage	ሻሽ፡ መጀነኒ፡ ባንደጅ
bruciarsi la mano	to burn one's hand	ኢድ ምንዳድ
cancro	cancer	ካንሰር
cerotto (adesivo)	(sticking) plaster	ፕላስተር
colpo di sole	sunstroke	ኮልቦዲሶለ
cotone idrofilo	cotton-wool	ብጡጥ ዝተሰርሐ ሱፍ
dentista (m/f)	dentist	ሓኪም ስኒ
diarrea	diarrhoea	ውጽኣት
dolore (m)	pain	ስቅያት፡ ቃንዛ
farmacia	chemist's (shop)	ቤት መድሃኒት
febbre (f)	fever, high temp.	ረስኒ
febbre da fieno	hay fever	ጉንፋዕ
ferito	wounded	ጉዱእ
guarire	to recover	ምድሓን
indigestione (f)	indigestion	ናይ ምሕቃቕ መግቢ ጸገማት
influenza	infuenza	እንፍልዌንዛ
ingessare	to put in plaster	ፕላስተር ምግባር
malattia	illness	ሕማም
mal di mare	sea-sickness	ሕማም ባሕሪ
medico	doctor	ሓኪም
medicina	medicine	መድሃኒት
mordere	to bite	ምንካስ
ospedale (m)	hospital	ሆስፒታል
otturazione (f)	filling	ምምላእ
pastiglia	tablet	ከኒና
pomata	ointment, cream	ፖማታ
pronto soccorso	first aid	ቀዳማይ ረድኤት
puntura	injection	መርፍእ ምውጋእ
raffreddato (essere...)	to have a cold	ሰዓል ምሕማም
ricetta	prescription	ትእዛዝ ሓኪም
salute (f)	health	ጥዕና
sanguinare	to bleed	ምድማይ
sciroppo	syrup, mixture	ሺሮቦ
tagliarsi	to cut	ምሕራድ
tosse (f)	cough	ሰዓል
vomitare	to vomit	ምምላስ (ተምላስ ምትፋእ)

Accident

(moto) ciclista	(motor) cyclist	ቺክሊስታ
aiutare	to help	ምሕጋዝ
all'improvviso	suddenly	ብሃንደበት
ambulanza	ambulance	ኣምቡላንስ
attenzione!	Look out!, Caution!	ተጠንቀቕ
attraversare	to cross	ምስጋር
autobus (m)	bus	ኣውቶቡስ
autocarro	lorry	ናይ ጽዕነት ማኪና
bruciare	to burn	ምንዳድ
cadere	to fall	ምውዳቕ
collisione (f)	collision	ግጭት
colpa	fault	ጌጋ
consolato	consulate	ቆንስል
correre	to run, to speed	ምጕያይ
corriera	coach	ኣውቶቡስ
danno	damage	ጕድኣት
fare attenzione	to be careful	ምጥንቃቕ
ferito	wounded	ጕዱእ
fuoco, (al ...!)	fire, (fire!)	ሓዊ (ሓዊ)
grave	serious	ዕቱብ
improvvisamente	suddenly	ሃንደበት
incidente (m)	accident	ድንገት
investire	to collide with, to run over	ምግጫው
macchina	car	መኪና
marciapiede (m)	pavement	ማርቻበዲ
morto	dead	ምዉት
passante (m/f)	passer-by	ሓላፍ መገዲ
pedone (m)	pedestrian	ኣጋር
pericolo	danger	ሓደጋ
polizia	police	ፖሊስ
presto!	quick!	ተሎ
scontro	collision, crash	ግጭት
senso unico	one way	እንኮ መሕለፊ
sorpassare	to overtake	ምሕላፍ
targa	number plate	ታርጋ
testimone (m/f)	witness	ምስክር
urto	collision, impact	ረጽሚ
vigili del fuoco	firemen	መጥፋእቲ ሓዊ

FREE TIME AND ENTERTAINMENT

andare a cavallo	to ride	ምግላብ
... in bicicletta	to cycle	ብሽክለታ ምዝዋር
... al mare	to go to the seaside	ገምገም ባሕሪ ምኻድ
... in campagna	... the countryside	ገጠር ምውጻእ
... in montagna	... the mountains	ጎቦ ምውጻእ
atletica	athletics	ኣትለቲክስ
attore (m)	actor	ተዋሳኣይ
ballare	to dance	ምስዕሳዕ
biblioteca	library	ቤት መጻሕፍቲ
calcio	football	ኵዕሶ እግሪ
camminare	to walk	ምኻድ
cantare	to sing	ምድራፍ
chitarra	guitar	ጊታር
ciclismo	cycling	ብሽክለታ ምዝዋር
cinema (m)	cinema	ሲነማ
collezionare	to collect	ውህለላ፡ ዝተዋጽአ
computer (m)	computer	ኮምፑዩተር
concerto	concert	ኮንሰርት
dama	draughts	ዳማ
discoteca	discotheque	ዲስኮተክ
fotografia	photography	ስእሊ
giocare a pallone	to play football	ኵዕሶ እግሪ ምጽዋት
leggere	to read	ምንባብ
museo	museum	ቤተ መዘክር
musica classica	classical music	ናይ ጥንቲ ብሉጽ ሙዚቃ
nuotare	to swim	ምሕንባስ
opera	opera	ኦፐራ
pallanuoto	water-polo	ኵዕሶ ማይ
pallacanestro	basket-ball	ኵዕሶ ሰኪዐት
pescare	to fish	ዓሳ ምግፋፍ
pianoforte (m)	piano	ፒያኖ
piscina	swimming pool	መሐንበሲ ማይ
rivista	magazine	መጽሔት
scacchi	chess	ቸስ
sciare	to ski	ምንሸርታት (ኣብ በረድ)
teatro	theatre	ትያትር
televisione (f)	television	ተለቪዥን
tennis (m)	tennis	ተኒስ

EDUCATION

General

alunno	pupil	ተመሃራይ
aula	classroom	ክፍሊ ቤት
banco	desk	ሰደቓ
biblioteca	library	ቤት መጻሕፍቲ
bocciare	to fail	ምውዳቕ፣ ምትራፍ
borsa di studio	grant, scholarship	ማህደረ ትምህርቲ
cattedra	teacher's desk	መንበረ መምህር
certificato	certificate	ምስክር ወረቐት
classe (f)	class	ክፍሊ
compito	homework	ናይ ገዛ ስራሕ
correggere	to correct, to mark	ምእራም
esame (m)	exam	ፈተና
frequentare	to attend	ምክትታል
gesso	chalk	ኩርሽ
gomma	rubber	መደምሰስ
imparare	to learn	ትምህርቲ ምቕሳም
insegnare	to teach	ምምሃር
intervallo	break	ዕረፍቲ
iscrizione (f)	enrolment	ምዝገባ
laurea	degree	ዲግሪ
lavagna	blackboard	ሰሌዳ
lezione (f)	lesson	ትምህርቲ (ኣብ ሓደ ኣርእስቲ)
libro	book	መጽሓፍ
maestro	(primary) teacher	መምህር
orario	timetable	ሰዓታት
preside (m/f)	headmaster/mistress	ርእሰ ሓላፊ/ሓላፊት
professore (m)	teacher, professor	መምህር
professoressa	teacher, professor	መምህር
promuovere	to pass	ምሕላፍ
quaderno	exercise book	ጥራዝ
sbaglio	mistake	ጌጋ (ልክዕ ዘይምዃን)
scrivere	to write	ምጽሓፍ
studente (m)	student	ተማሃራይ
studentessa (f)	student	ተማሃሪት
studiare	to study	ምጽናዕ
uniforme	uniform	ዩኒፎርም፣ ዲቪዛ
università	university	ዩኒቨርሲቲ

Subjects

arabo	Arabic	ዓረብ
biologia	biology	ባዮሎጂ
ceramica	pottery	ስራሕ ካይላ
chimica	chemistry	ኬሚስትሪ
dattilografia	typing	ጽሕፈት መኪና
economia	economics	ስነ ቍጠባ
educazione artistica	art	ስነጥበብ
educazione fisica	physical education	ትምህርቲ ምውስዋስ አካላት
educazione musicale	music	ሙዚቃ
elettronica	electronics	ኤለክትሮኒክስ
fisica	physics	ፊዚክስ
francese (m)	French	ፈረንሳ
geografia	geography	ሕብረ-ትምህርቲ (ጂኦግራፊ)
greco	Greek	ትምህርቲ ቋንቋ ግሪኽ
informatica	computer science	ኮምፕዩተር
inglese (m)	English	እንግሊዝ
italiano	Italian	ጣልያን
latino	Latin	ላቲን
letteratura	literature	ስነ ጽሑፍ
lingue moderne	modern languages	ዘመናዊ ቋንቋ
matematica	maths	ቍጽሪ
morale (f)	ethics	ሞራላዊ ትምህርቲ
musica	music	ሙዚቃ
ragioneria	accounting	ኣካውንቲን (ሕሳብ)
religione (f)	religious education	ትምህርቲ ሃይማኖት
scienze (f, pl.)	science	ሳይንስ
scienze naturali	natural sciences	ተፈጥሮኣዊ ሳይንስ
scienze umane	human sciences	ባህርያዊ ሳይንስ
sociologia	sociology	መጽናዕቲ ሕብረተሰብ
spagnolo	Spanish	ስጳኛ
stenografia	shorthand	ቅልጣፈ ጽሕፈት ብኣሕጽሮት ቃላት
storia dell'arte	history of art	ታሪኽ ስነ ጥበብ
storia	history	ታሪኽ
teatro	drama	ድራማ
tedesco	German	ጀርመን
tigrino	Tigrinya	ትግርኛ